How to Launch an
Author Awards Program
at Your Library

HOW TO LAUNCH AN AUTHOR AWARDS PROGRAM AT YOUR LIBRARY

CURATING SELF-PUBLISHED BOOKS, REACHING OUT TO THE COMMUNITY

Julianne Stam and Elizabeth Clemmons,
EDITORS

LIBRARIES
UNLIMITED™
An Imprint of ABC-CLIO, LLC
Santa Barbara, California • Denver, Colorado

Library of Congress Cataloging-in-Publication Data

Names: Stam, Julianne, editor | Clemmons, Elizabeth, editor.

Title: How to launch an author awards program at your library : curating self-published books, reaching out to the community / Julianne Stam and Elizabeth Clemmons, editors.

Description: Santa Barbara, CA : Libraries Unlimited, [2016] | Includes bibliographical references and index.

Identifiers: LCCN 2015031402| ISBN 9781440841644 (paperback) | ISBN 9781440841651 (ebook)

Subjects: LCSH: Libraries—Cultural programs—Handbooks, manuals, etc. | Libraries and community—Handbooks, manuals, etc. | Libraries—Marketing—Handbooks, manuals, etc. | Reading promotion—Handbooks, manuals, etc. | Self-publishing—United States. | Libraries and electronic publishing—United States. | Authors and readers. | Libraries—Cultural programs—Illinois—Case studies. | BISAC: LANGUAGE ARTS & DISCIPLINES / Library & Information Science / General. | LANGUAGE ARTS & DISCIPLINES / Library & Information Science / Administration & Management.

Classification: LCC Z716.4 .H69 2016 | DDC 021.2/6—dc23

LC record available at http://lccn.loc.gov/2015031402

ISBN: 978-1-4408-4164-4
EISBN: 978-1-4408-4165-1

20 19 18 17 16   1 2 3 4 5

This book is also available on the World Wide Web as an eBook.
Visit www.abc-clio.com for details.

Libraries Unlimited
An Imprint of ABC-CLIO, LLC

ABC-CLIO, LLC
130 Cremona Drive, P.O. Box 1911
Santa Barbara, California 93116-1911

This book is printed on acid-free paper ∞
Manufactured in the United States of America

CONTENTS

Foreword   vii
David Vinjamuri

Preface: What is the Soon to be Famous Illinois Author Project?   ix
Sue Wilsey

Acknowledgments   xiii

Introduction   xv
Elizabeth Clemmons

**Chapter 1: Break Away from Normal—Get Going on Soon
to be Famous: The Why Chapter**   **1**
Denise Raleigh

Chapter 2: Project Formation   **11**
Christine Niels Cigler

Chapter 3: Getting Others Involved in the Project   **23**
Denise Raleigh

**Chapter 4: Communicating with Authors, Accepting
Submissions, and the Polar Vortex**   **35**
Donna Fletcher

Chapter 5: Judging the Nominated Books   **41**
Julianne Stam

Chapter 6: The Final Three and the Big Announcement   **67**
Anita Quinlan

Chapter 7: Promoting the Winner (or Almost Famous)   **73**
Nicole Zimmermann

Chapter 8: Going Forward   **87**
Lucy Tarabour

Afterword   93
Lucy Tarabour

Appendix A: Project Timeline and Documentation 95
Julianne Stam

Appendix B: Writing a Book Review 109
Julianne Stam

Appendix C: Library Marketing Guidelines and Resources 111
Denise Raleigh

Appendix D: Creating a Marketing Plan for Your Author Contest 127
Christine Niels Cigler

Appendix E: A Short History of Self-Publishing 129
Elizabeth Clemmons

Appendix F: The First Soon to be Famous Illinois Author—
The Movie 131
Joanne Zienty

Index 137

About the Editors and Contributors 141

FOREWORD

David Vinjamuri

What the Illinois librarians who created the Soon to be Famous Illinois Author Project have done is nothing short of remarkable. They've taken the first step toward changing the balance of power between libraries and publishers and reinventing the library for the next generation. Let me explain.

I became involved with libraries by accident. In the early fall of 2012, I was approached by two women who had started a small publishing house devoted to nontraditional tween titles. They'd just been fortunate enough to get one of their books featured on a national morning television show. Then they had a brilliant idea to promote the book. They decided to donate one electronic copy of the book to every public library in America. And then they hit a wall.

The dominant provider of eBooks to libraries told this small publisher that it was too small to deal with—in spite of the national exposure the authors' book had just received. And also in spite of the fact that they were trying to *give away the book for free*, not sell it.

In frustration, these women approached me. I spent over 15 years as a marketer, with stints at Johnson & Johnson, Coca-Cola, and other large companies, before I started teaching at New York University and contributing to *Forbes*. I had just written an article about self-publishing and how it was changing the landscape of the publishing industry. These two women had read that article and contacted me because they thought something was going on with libraries that I might want to write about.

I was interested in their story and began to investigate. Just at that time, Maureen Sullivan—then president of the American Library Association—wrote an open letter to publishers, detailing the frustrations that libraries were experiencing with eBooks. I learned from Maureen that many eBooks that were cheaply available to ordinary citizens could not be had from publishers at any price. For others, the price was dear: $84 or more for a book that a Kindle reader could purchase for $9.99 or less.

My intent was to write a short article commenting on these practices from a marketer's point of view. Instead, fascinated by what I learned, I wrote two pieces for *Forbes* totaling over 10,000 words. Nearly 300,000 people read those articles online.

So it was that the American Library Association invited me to speak at its annual conference in Chicago in 2013. I was nervous because it was a Sunday morning at 8:00, and there were an intimidating 175 seats to be filled. On the day, however, librarians started pouring in early—so many that 50 or more had to be turned away, and we counted 250 in the room, sitting, standing, and lounging on the floor.

I told the librarians that I was shocked by the attitude of publishers toward libraries. As a teacher of social media, I wondered aloud why it was that people were still reading at all. In a world with Facebook, television, Netflix, video games, iPhones, and so many other distractions, how was reading still flourishing? I looked back to 1450, when the Gutenberg press made reading more affordable for more people. Virtually every other popular pastime of that era is no more than a curiosity today. (Try to find a good shin-kicking, fox hunt, or public execution to while away your time on a quiet Saturday afternoon these days!)

I speculated that it is libraries' commitments to early childhood reading that has kept reading alive for each subsequent generation in America. So without libraries, publishers would quite literally be out of business. I told the librarians gathered in that room that as a consumer marketer, I would have been thrilled to have access to something dedicated to my products and happy to display my products without charging me for the privilege. That if I were a publisher, I'd send displays of new authors and use their patrons to build a name for these writers.

There was a lot of excitement in that room, and both the librarians and I left the conference energized. That was great and a little surprising. But what happened next was even more surprising. Before I was five feet out of the door to the room, several Illinois librarians approached me. One of the things I had suggested that libraries ought to do was to evaluate a bunch of self-published books, find one they liked, and then promote it. I told them that if they could create best sellers entirely outside the traditional publishing system, they'd turn the tables on publishers.

These Illinois librarians took me at my word and set out to do exactly that. They created the Soon to be Famous Illinois Author competition, and to date they have run that competition twice, gaining both local and national attention in the process. In addition, the model is spreading to other states.

Don't mistake what these dedicated library professionals are doing as simply a contest or a way to deal with the large number of self-published authors looking for a simple way of engaging with their libraries. Soon to be Famous goes even further. It seeks to reestablish the library as the best place to find new voices. It provides a direct channel between local authors and local readers, just as a farm-to-table restaurant might. And it's the first skirmish in a much bigger war: to reestablish libraries as the first and most important partners of the publishing industry.

PREFACE:
WHAT IS THE SOON
TO BE FAMOUS ILLINOIS
AUTHOR PROJECT?

Sue Wilsey

One of the most widely shared pair of articles via library blogs and Facebook feeds in early 2013 was a two-part series from *Forbes* contributor David Vinjamuri. "The Wrong War Over eBooks: Publishers Vs. Libraries" and "Why Public Libraries Matter: And How They Can Do More" essentially made the case that public "libraries should cooperate to discover great books" (Vinjamuri, 2012, 2013).

So when Vinjamuri was scheduled in the way-too-early-for-a-Sunday-morning slot on June 30 at the 2013 American Library Association conference in Chicago for a presentation entitled "The $84 Question: Why Libraries Matter and Can Do More in the Era of E-books, Social Media and Branding," he drew a standing-room-only audience. Among the attendees were a group of closely networked local library marketers who enthusiastically embraced his challenge to libraries to wield their collective influence to make a self-published author a success. The hope was to create a measurable indicator of the power of libraries and librarians to affect books and reading.

In a period of just a few months, the ambitious (some would say insane) group coined the title of the Soon to be Famous Illinois Author Project, created a logo design, set up a Facebook page and Web site, and secured a booth and presentation for the October 2013 Illinois Library Association Conference, and the project was under way. The team agreed on certain parameters for the project: author nominations would be accepted only from Illinois libraries, participating authors would be Illinois residents, and accepted works would be adult fiction and must be self-published.

More than 20 professional librarians across the state volunteered to act as judges. By the time the deadline for the project rolled around in January 2014, after some nice media publicity generated by the Soon to be Famous (STBF) team, 103 authors had been nominated. Three rounds of judging led to three finalists and the announcement of the winner at a major media event during National Library Week in April 2014. Vinjamuri, who provided great support for the project throughout, was in attendance at that event to announce the winner.

The STBF Project is an example of disruptive innovation of a well-established process of collection development, which relies almost exclusively on the offerings of the Big Five publishers. But in the new era of eBooks, the pricing structure and distribution model have been out of whack, hence Vinjamuri's $84 question, which referred to the average cost per book that libraries were being charged for a single eBook license, versus the significantly lower cost per book charged to individual consumers.

Libraries had previously looked at the self-published model as an alternative when print-on-demand (POD) services like AuthorHouse, iUniverse, and Xlibris appeared in the middle and late 1990s. This model appealed to authors who were frustrated by repeated rejections from major and independent publishers.

Always on the lookout for new titles, libraries initially felt a responsibility to take a strong interest in this new source of materials. But when newspapers declined to review these POD books, and booksellers were reluctant to stock them, libraries reconsidered this approach. And it did not help that so many of these books were just not well written or edited (Dilevko & Dali, 2006, pp. 208–234).

According to David Streitfeld in "Amazon Offers All You Can Eat Books," "the world now has more stories than it needs or wants to pay for. In 2010, Amazon had 600,000 e-books in its Kindle store. Today it has more than three million. The number of books on Smashwords, which distributes self-published writers, grew 20 percent in 2013" (2014).

However, multiple professional reviews are usually a criterion for most librarians to consider adding a book to their collections, and much self-published material has not been reviewed.

And while a company like Smashwords begins experimenting with recommendation lists based on title popularity and SELF-e, a joint venture between the digital content delivery platform BiblioBoard and *Library Journal*, provides a curated collection of eBooks, the Soon to be Famous Project process can be duplicated by library systems in states and regions across the county.

REFERENCES

Dali, K., & Dilevko, J. (2006). *Library & Information Science Research*, 28 208–234.

Streitfeld, D. (2014, December 27). Amazon offers all you can eat books: Authors turn up noses. *The New York Times*. Retrieved from http://www.nytimes.com/2014/12/28/technology/amazon-offers-all-you-can-eat-books-authors-turn-up-noses.html?_r=0

Vinjamuri, David. (2012, December 11). The wrong war over eBooks: Publishers vs. libraries (blog). *Forbes*. Retrieved from http://www.forbes.com/sites/davidvinjamuri /2012/12/11/the-wrong-war-over-ebooks-publishers-vs-libraries/

Vinjamuri, David. (2013, January 6). Why public libraries matter: And how they can do more. *Forbes*. Retrieved from http://www.forbes.com/sites/davidvinjamuri/2013/01/16 /why-public-libraries-matter-and-how-they-can-do-more/

Acknowledgments

In this truly collaborative project, there were many people behind the scenes whose contributions we appreciate—from creating the logo to directing the videos, from judging books to designing posters—we couldn't have done this without you.

LIBRARY DIRECTORS

Betsy Adamowski, Leslie Bednar, Roxane Bennett, Jamie Bukovac, Lori Craft, Jeannie Dilger, Melissa Gardner, Nann Blaine Hilyard, Karen Kleckner Keefe, Barb Kruser, Karen Danczak Lyons, Carole Medal, Ron Stoch, Gwen Stupar, Linda Weiss, and Stacy Wittmann.

2014 JUDGES

Renee Buker, Tish Calhamer, Rachel Dabkey, Brian Grega, Debbie Hoffman, Elizabeth Hopkins, Rebecca Malinowski, Elsie Martinez, Jennie Milojevic, Tracey Nielsen, Lynnanne Pearson, Jessica Perham, Shauna Porteus, Christine Sporleder, Johnna Schultz, Becky Spratford, Kelli Staley, Julie Stielstra, Marlise Schiltz, Magan Szwarek, Carly Thompson, Heather Ventucci-Johnson, and John Wallace.

2015 JUDGES

Laura Berkley, Beth Bozzo, Judith M. Brannigan, Tish Calhamer, Linda Conrath, Jolie Duncan, Jane Easterly, Susan R. Franzen, Nann Blaine Hilyard, Robin Helenthal, Liza Hickey, Nancy Huntley, Sarah Kovac, Johnna Schultz, Christine Sporleder, Kelli Staley, Eve Stano, and Julie Stielstra

OTHER BRILLIANT CONTRIBUTORS

Mary Amici-Kozi, David Bunn, Brett Butcher, Tish Calhamer, Chris Clark, Daniel Escamilla, Laura Espinoza, Jane Hartney, Joan Hull, Deb Huffman, Sara Johnson, Karen McBride, Betsy O'Connell, Theresa Papaurelis, Veronda Pitchford, Margaret Peebles, Deirdre Thurman, Natalie Williams, and Tyler Works.

SPECIAL THANKS

Dee Brennan, executive director of RAILS (Reaching Across Illinois Library System), and Bob Doyle, executive director of ILA (Illinois Library Association), were undeniably instrumental to the success of this project. They enthusiastically supported our efforts from the very beginning, generously sharing resources and offering encouragement. We truly could not have done this without them. David Vinjamuri, the person who sparked the idea for this whole project, deserves special thanks too. We would likely never have tried this if he hadn't suggested doing it.

INTRODUCTION

Elizabeth Clemmons

No cigars were passed out, but congratulations were proclaimed to the proud parents—all eight of them—and to their baby, the Soon to be Famous Illinois Author Project, when the first winner was announced on April 16, 2014. Conceived nine months earlier at a library conference and nurtured with collaboration and creativity, the project was not without some growing pains. Much like its human counterpart, it caused conflicting emotions for its parents, who alternated between excited anticipation and stressful apprehension about the possible outcome of this new creation.

The Soon to be Famous Project was developed by library marketing professionals who liked the ideas of both supporting self-published authors and getting the message to traditional book publishers that libraries and librarians greatly influence readers' choices. As marketers, Denise, Donna, Cris, Julie, Sue, Nikki, Anita, and Liz are used to multitasking, making decisions on the fly, communicating effectively to different types of audiences, brainstorming to come up with new ways to make ideas stick, and collaborating with many different people on the same project, not to mention rolling up their sleeves and digging in.

The committee faced two issues that have discouraged other fledgling projects. At the outset, most of the STBF committee members did not know each other well. And the libraries at which they worked were scattered over a great distance in the Chicago area. These marketers made it happen and got to know each other well enough to laugh together—and laugh often!

All eight brought many different talents to the table. Like many who work in public libraries, these marketers had had other previous careers like lawyer, teacher, journalist, and advertising executive. But despite their differences, all eight are passionate about libraries. They believe libraries are essential to our communities, providing opportunities for literacy, learning, and fun as well as supporting Soon to be Famous Authors!

ABOUT THIS BOOK

This book assembles the experts who "were there" to offer you detailed instructions on how you and your library can enter the new and exciting arena of librarian-curated self-publishing. Although the Soon to be Famous Project was conceived and executed by public librarians, we believe the model can be adopted and adapted to any type of library.

Chapters cover every step of the process, from explaining exactly what librarian-curated self-publishing is, why you should get involved in it, and how to get organized, recruit others to help, solicit submissions, deal with authors, and judge books, to announcing and promoting the winners and assessing the outcomes.

More than a guide to how libraries can establish an award program for self-published work, this book also provides librarians with a new way to bolster their relevance and expand upon their role as curators and "keepers of story." It is a great way to engage community. It is our sincere hope that within these pages you find the inspiration and practical advice you need for launching an author awards program.

1

BREAK AWAY FROM NORMAL—GET GOING ON SOON TO BE FAMOUS: THE WHY CHAPTER

Denise Raleigh

This chapter is the "Ah-hah, I get it!" chapter. Many of you are anxious to skip to the enlightening "how you can do it, too" chapters, but this section will give you interesting statistics and citations that will clearly prove why you should sweep away that boring project that has been gathering dust on your desk (you really did not want to do it anyway) and move quickly forward on the Soon to be Famous (STBF) project in your community. You can use what you learn here as ammunition to get others just as excited as you are about this project.

A huge element of this cutting-edge project is that it is about librarian expertise, library crowdsourcing, and library power. As described in the introduction, many library folks were extremely energized about library staff working to make an obscure author famous to prove library power after hearing David Vinjamuri speak at the annual American Library Association conference in 2013. As this book is being written, the publishers may be starting to respect libraries a little more, and pricing by the Big Five publishers may be heading to a commonsense place, but this project is amazing even without the underlying "you done me wrong" fuel.

In a nutshell, an author awards project entails library staff nominating self-published authors from their community. All of the "how-tos" of this process are outlined in chapters 2 through 8. Basically, professional librarians from the community judge the submissions, and the author to be made famous is selected. One absolutely essential element of this project, which must be included without fail, is fun. Meeting new people—librarians, library staffers,

Figure 1.1. Watch *It's a Writingful Life* at http://www.youtube.com/watch?v=RgjAvSBkoKg&feature=youtu.be.

authors, media, and members of the public—is an awesome component. (Please take time to watch the parody *It's a Writingful Life* [see figure 1.1], which involved many Illinois librarians.) As you might imagine, there will be all manner of self-published submissions by a wonderfully unique array of authors, all with stories of their own. Also to be encountered will be people with a wide variety of views about self-publishing and how things should be done as they were in the past. Our project changed some minds, creating new connections along the way, and hopefully yours will, too.

THIS IS WHAT LIBRARIES CAN DO

According to *History Magazine*, "the Great Library of Alexandria, a public library open to those with the proper scholarly and literary qualifications, was founded about 300 BC" (Krasner-Khait, 2001). When Egypt's King Ptolemy I (305–282 BC) asked, "How many scrolls do we have?" Aristotle's disciple, Demetrius of Phalerum, was on hand to answer with the latest count. After all, it was Demetrius who suggested setting up a universal library to hold copies of all the books in the world. Ptolemy and his successors wanted to understand the people under their rule and to house Latin, Buddhist, Persian, Hebrew, and Egyptian works—all translated into Greek.

The library's lofty goal was to collect a half a million scrolls, and the Ptolemies took serious steps to accomplish that. Ptolemy I, for example, composed a letter to all the sovereigns and governors he knew, imploring them "not to hesitate to send him works by authors of every kind" (Krasner-Khait, 2001).

When scrolls were scarce, libraries housed them to benefit everyone. Nowadays the number of "scrolls" is exploding. The library consumer not only wants to read the scrolls; he or she also wants to create them.

When Johannes Gutenberg mechanized the printed book, libraries added books to their collections of scrolls. In 2011 Fred Lerner wrote: "By 1500 . . . tens of thousands of titles had been published" (p. 84).

In 2015 many libraries are all about maker spaces, where people can build objects. Have these spaces been exciting and provocative? Yes. But we should also be maker spaces for our core product, books. According to David Vinjamuri (2013), in 2012 there were 391,768 self-published books, 270,743 eBooks traditionally published, and 316,190 books traditionally published.

LIBRARIES ARE ABOUT BOOKS

"The library brand—it's still BOOK." This was one of the major findings of the 2011 Online Computer Library Center (OCLC) study, *Perceptions of Libraries, 2010: Context and Community* (De Rosa et al., 2011). As virtually all library folks know (but it bears emphasizing), most of our visitors come to borrow books. No matter how many additional services we add, like maker spaces and passport services, we still are about books.

When David Vinjamuri engages us in his inspiring presentations, he speaks about how libraries have been the keystone to keeping reading number one in recreation for centuries, even after the onslaught of technology that has provided myriad choices to everyone. Even though books were invented thousands of years ago, we should be pretty darn proud and happy that these wonderful compilations that have transformed the world and provided multitudes with great recreation are still so popular.

As the prolific teaching librarian S. R. Ranganathan noted in his five laws:

Books are for use.
Every reader, his book.
Every book, its reader.
Save the time of the reader.
A library is a growing organism. (Cloonan & Dove, 2005)

Finding good reads for people is fundamental to the mission of libraries. The factors that Samuel Green, who crafted many of the first fundamental library philosophies regarding reference and community relationships in the late 1800s, wrote about more than 100 years ago are still the cornerstones of library work: teaching people to use the library, answering questions, advising customers regarding reading selections, and promoting the library in the community (Bopp & Smith, 2011).

Self-published books can no longer be ignored by libraries, lest we remain in the "world is flat" culture of narrowly defining what a book is. In 2014 Betty Sargent of *Publishers Weekly* presented compelling statistics from the "Author Earnings" report, indicating that this compilation was generated from "7,000 top selling digital genre titles on Amazon's category bestseller lists." Among its findings were the following:

- The Big Five traditional publishers now account for only 16 percent of the eBooks on Amazon's best-seller lists.

- Self-published books now represent 31 percent of eBook sales at Amazon's Kindle store.
- Indie authors are earning nearly 40 percent of the eBook dollars going to authors.
- Self-published authors are "dominating traditionally published authors" in sci-fi/fantasy, mystery/thriller, and romance genres, but—and here is the surprise—they are also taking "significant market share in all genres."

KEEPING READING ALIVE AND LIBRARIES RELEVANT

Business writer Brian Solis uses the phrase "digital Darwinism" when he answers the question: "What killed Borders, Blockbuster and Polaroid?" (2013). Of course he is talking about leaders who do not react to consumer trends fast enough. Solis wrote in a recent blog post that, "Over the years, I've studied how disruptive technology affects consumer behavior and decision-making. I've also researched how businesses react (or don't) to these changes. What I've learned is that barring a few exceptional instances of complete ignorance, organizations are open to adaptation if there's indeed a case made for it and a path outlined to safely and cost-effectively navigate change."

Libraries have shown a keen ability to adapt throughout the years. From the scroll to the Gutenberg press, from the card catalog to online catalogs and Google, librarians have helped people find good reads no matter the format or whether or not they come from a Big Five publishing house.

Change has come. As early as October 2010, Amazom.com's Kindle eBooks outsold best-selling print books two to one (De Rosa et al., 2011). *Information World Review* reports that "an analysis of US ISBN data reveals that the number of self-published titles in 2012 was 391,000[,] up 59% over 2011 and 422% over 2007. The analysis by Bowker, an affiliate of ProQuest, shows that eBooks continued to gain on print[,] comprising 40% of the ISBNs that were self-published in 2012, up from just 11% in 2007."

Another element of the 2010 OCLC perception study that needs emphasis is that the youngest survey group holds the strongest library book brand perception. The OCLC report indicates that libraries are valued and that people are using library services. It shows that we in the industry have plenty of opportunity to improve. In marketing parlance, the customers you already have are the most valuable to keep and serve. Quite simply, library customers read books.

Ranganathan's laws are more important than ever in the world in which we provide library services. With the gap between the haves and have-nots widening, libraries often provide the only access with expert assistance for many people in need. Library budgets everywhere are under downward pressure, meaning that materials that we invest in should be used. Time is now the scarcest of commodities, and change is happening faster than ever before. STBF is all about helping people find good reads and working together to cull through the vast amount of self-published material to find material for collections and, ultimately, our library patrons.

When Ranganathan espoused his third law, he was impressed that people could go in the stacks to find a book and discover another book they'd like to read. Libraries can and should do the same thing with their resources that are offered in an electronic form. Amazon and other retailers have adopted algorithms that suggest to a visitor, "if you were looking at this, you may also like that." StumbleUpon, a Web site that refers on subjects based on user-selected interests, has 20 million users based on people's love for referrals. These types of add-ons are slowly making their way into library catalogs, but the online catalog vendors have been slow to adopt these innovations, and they are often costly when they do offer a product. Author awards programs are all about providing another avenue for finding a good read.

As library professionals, we have to study our customers. All of Ranganathan's laws speak to maximizing library usage. As noted in Sargent's statement that 40 percent of eBook dollars are going to indie authors, readers are seeking self-published books. Libraries need to be part of this process.

COLLECTION DEVELOPMENT, LIBRARY CROWDSOURCING STYLE

As *Information World Review* reported, the number of self-published books is exploding, with 391,000 in 2012 ("US self-publishing movement," 2013). In addition, as Sargent (2014) indicated, people are reading self-published books in increasing numbers. Vinjamuri (2013) notes that libraries have to consider self-published books as they win major awards and become more sought after among readers.

In 2013 Josh Hadro, the executive editor of *Library Journal*, observed that the problems with collection development and self-published books were quality and quantity: "Partially to deflect the stigma associated with self-publishing, libraries historically developed collection policies asking authors to supply independent proof of a title's appeal. As Ted Bohaczuk, orders librarian at the Free Library of Philadelphia (FLP), describes it, 'We have a soft response that says, "We base our purchasing decisions to a large extent on reviews that are available, please attempt to get your product reviewed"; the FLP practice is to advise authors that 'as your title gets reviews, we will make a determination as the budget permits'" (p. 34).

STBF is not going to create a huge number of recommended self-published books, but it is a way for libraries to get a taste of the world to come.

LIBRARIES AS EDUCATIONAL HUBS

In 2012 Sue Roberts of the State Library of Victoria wrote about how libraries are shifting from lending to learning, now that technology has become much more consumer friendly and accessible: "Libraries must continue to develop and evolve their role in the learning landscape in order to have a significant impact on learners, learning, social inclusion, educational attainment, and employment outcomes. In order to do this they must continually remind themselves that 'It's not about us; it's about them' and put learners, their diverse needs and aspirations, at the heart of their vision, strategies, programs and services" (p. 159).

An author award project is filled with educational opportunity. Following are just some of the questions that we answered on a continual basis:

- I have not finished my book, but would you read it and provide feedback?
- How does an author become self-published?
- I need to find a writers' group. Do you know where I can find one?
- How do you submit a book to Amazon?
- How do you submit a book to Smashwords?
- What is the difference between Amazon and Smashwords?
- How do I copyright a book?
- I am an author; who do I connect with at my local library?

Involvement in an author awards program will increase all of the committee members' working knowledge about self-published books. It will also highlight the fact that there is a deep need for libraries to assist authors. Libraries and authors indeed continue to be joined at the hip.

WHEN LIBRARY PEOPLE GET TOGETHER

MacLeod wrote about the Library at Alexandria as being collaborative in nature, stating that it "would welcome learned Greeks to come together and work together, to pursue mathematics and medicine, literature and poetry, physics and philosophy" (2004, p. 3).

Libraries are all about collaboration. Bringing books together for people to borrow is all about a collaborative community. The history of libraries is awash with good results when libraries get together. Because libraries joined forces, we have worldwide catalogs, interlibrary loans, shared databases, and collective professionalism. This project brought a number of people together from libraries across the state for a common good: choosing an excellent Illinois author to promote.

Another key positive that results from an author awards project is stronger connections between libraries, between libraries and authors, and between libraries and media. The core committee members of STBF's first year were representatives from six different libraries and a consulting firm. Two more great people from two additional libraries now are heavy contributors. Most of us knew one or two others. Now, we have new good friends. The work brought stronger connections to our associations, both the

Reaching Across Illinois Library System and the Illinois Library Association. We have had strong support from the Heartland Library System in downstate Illinois, the Digital Content Working Group of the American Library Association, and the Public Library Association.

The judging committee was made up of Illinois professional librarians from 20 different libraries. (See figure 1.2.) The project received nominations from libraries across the state. STBF brought people from across Illinois together.

Figure 1.2. STBF received nominations from libraries across the state.

GETTING LOCAL: STBF BROUGHT LIBRARIES TOGETHER WITH THEIR LOCAL AUTHORS

As the STBF project moved forward, we recognized that there was no uniformity among libraries regarding dealing with authors. Some libraries had well-established writers' groups in which new members were reviewed. Some libraries had no writers' group. Some had writing groups that were informal, where people could go to read their works.

An author awards project motivates writers to contact their local libraries, where they will be met mostly with open arms. Some libraries may purchase copies from the new authors with whom they come in contact. Yes, there will be a few libraries that do not embrace the idea, but a contact will be created. And hopefully next year that same library will accept that author's nomination and purchase that local book.

LANDING THE VALUE MESSAGE FOR CREATING MARKETS

An author awards program is a recipe for landing the library value message. It is taking a core function—recommending quality books to patrons—from start to finish, the whole time highlighting the expertise in our libraries. In the case of STBF, the value message was spread by two major Illinois newspapers reporting on the first STBF winner.

Annemarie Mannion of the *Chicago Tribune* wrote on December 31, 2013:

> In addition to bringing acclaim to a writer laboring in obscurity, librarians sponsored the contest in hopes of making the country's top publishers take notice of their power to be literary tastemakers by connecting books with

readers. It's part of an effort to nudge top publishers to change prices and policies on selling e-books to libraries, practices that librarians say limit the ability of patrons to borrow. (p. 5)

The *Daily Herald* reported on April 22, 2014:

Zienty was announced winner for her book *The Things We Save* at an award ceremony held last week at the Reaching Across Illinois Libraries (RAILS) headquarters in Burr Ridge. Librarians served as judges for a contest in which 103 self-published adult fiction authors competed, according to the Illinois Library Association. (Des Plaines librarian, 2014)

STBF is all about library professionals helping to create a channel of good reads, more relationships, and great value messages, and having tons of fun along the way. Keep reading to find out how you can CREATE YOUR OWN STBF PROJECT to do it, too.

REFERENCES

Bopp, R. E., & Smith, L. C. (2011). *Reference and information services: An introduction.* (4th ed.). Santa Barbara, CA: Libraries Unlimited.

Cloonan, M. V., & Dove, J. G. (2005). Ranganathan online. *Library Journal, 130*(6), 58–60.

De Rosa, C., Cantrell, J., Carlson, M., Gallagher, P., Hawk, J., & Sturtz, C. (2011). *Perceptions of libraries, 2010, context and community: A report to the OCLC membership.* Dublin, OH: OCLC.

Des Plaines librarian wins "Soon to be famous" author award. (2014, April 22). *Daily Herald Report*, April 22, 2014. Retrieved from http://www.dailyherald.com/article/20140422/news/140429528/

Hadro, J. (2013). What's the problem with self-publishing? *Library Journal, 138*(7), 34.

Krasner-Khait, B. (2001, October/November). Survivor: The history of the library. *History Magazine*. Retrieved from http://www.history-magazine.com/libraries.html

Lerner, F. A. (2011). *The story of libraries, from the invention of writing to the computer age.* New York: Continuum International Publishing Group.

MacLeod, R. M. (2004). *The Library of Alexandria: Centre of learning in the ancient world.* London: I. B. Tauris.

Mannion, A. (2013, December 31). Illinois library contest aimed at changing e-book policies: Lenders want publishers to ease restrictions, adjust pricing. *Chicago Tribune*, p. 5.

Roberts, S. (2012). Our learning landscape: Opportunities, challenges and possibilities. *Aplis, 25*(4), 156–160.

Sargent, B. (2014). Surprising self-publishing stats. *Publishers Weekly, 261*(34), 61.

Solis, B. (2013, February 27). *Digital Darwinism: What killed Borders, Blockbuster and Polaroid and how to survive.* Retrieved from https://www.linkedin.com/pulse/article/20130227142546-2293140-digital-darwinism-what-killed-borders-blockbuster-and-polaroid-and-how-not-to-end-up-like-them

US self-publishing movement continues strong growth. (2013). *Information World Review*, 5, p. 5.

Vinjamuri, D. (2013). The $84 question: Why libraries matter and can do more in the era of e-books, social media and branding. PR Forum 2013, American Library Association Annual Conference, Chicago, IL.

2

PROJECT FORMATION

Christine Niels Cigler

Deciding whether to hold an author awards contest is just the first of many decisions you'll have to make. Our experience launching the Soon to be Famous Illinois Author Project can serve as a model, but there are areas that you may want to customize. Your specific circumstances, perhaps the strength of library organizations, availability of volunteers, and the awareness of eBook pricing and self-publishing issues, as well as the time frame, will help shape the parameters of your contest.

FORMING THE TEAM

There are two approaches to putting together a team to work on a project like the Soon to be Famous (STBF) Author Project. You can strategically recruit people who have specific talents that would benefit the project, or you could simply put out a call for volunteers. Conceivably, you could work with any librarians interested in the concept; you could reach out to special interest groups such as readers' advisors, book selectors, book discussion leaders, and library directors. Reaching out to a special interest group for volunteers combines both approaches. In our case, we reached out to marketing colleagues.

Our project started in the afterglow of an especially inspiring presentation by *Forbes* writer David Vinjamuri at the 2013 ALA Annual Conference (Vinjamuri, 2013). Those of us who were at the presentation started brainstorming immediately. Soon after, we contacted Reaching Across Illinois Libraries System (RAILS), which covers the northern half of Illinois, and sought its support, which it offered on the spot. Within a few days, we were discussing our project at the RAILS Marketing Group meeting in July and asked if anyone wanted to join us.

Later that month, the Illinois Library Association had its annual orientation session. Several of us were on the ILA marketing committee, and we reached out to that group. The committee agreed to lend its support, and several of the members became core members of the first STBF committee. We presented the idea to the entire leadership of the ILA, including all committee chairs and their members, later that day. We garnered feedback, support, and additional volunteers. Ultimately, the inaugural committee was composed of marketing professionals from libraries in the greater Chicagoland area committed to the challenge of demonstrating the value of libraries and librarians in keeping the culture of reading alive. Once we got together, the ideas flew fast and furious.

Who Is Doing What?

Approaching an undertaking like this means implementing solid project management skills, including setting a timeline and assigning responsibilities. You may even consider assigning one person as a committee chair or coordinator so that there is always someone who is aware of what's happening in all areas of the project and can keep track of deadlines and follow up on details.

Ideally, managing a project of this scope would entail assigning a person to be responsible for specific areas of the project, such as the following:

- Press releases—assign these to a good writer with press connections to handle all of them.
- Press clippings—if you can, assign someone to track and save any press coverage, in newspapers, professional publications, blogs, and Web sites.
- Social media—someone with social media expertise could manage Facebook, Twitter, and other postings.
- Photographer—a decent photographer could be charged with taking and organizing photos.
- Author coordinator—someone who is good with detail work could coordinate all the details of tracking author submissions, contact information, etc.
- Note-taker/secretary—task one member with note taking, memorializing decisions that the committee makes. While discussions of meetings do not need to be detailed, a list of decisions made, dates agreed on, and deadlines should be kept and disseminated.
- Event coordinator—someone can schedule and coordinate all the details of appearing at conventions, meetings, etc.
- Marketing—someone can prepare flyers, posters, handouts, banners, and bookmarks; maintain the brand; and target audiences.
- Partnership coordinator—task someone with reaching out to various groups and organizations and managing contact information and commitments.
- Judge liaison—have someone recruit judges and coordinate the flow of books and reviews.
- Web site manager—have someone keep the Web site up to date.
- Document manager—A huge decision that will affect how easily the group can share information is choosing a format for document sharing. Whether it's Dropbox or Google Drive or some other Web-based service, get it started early and have someone in charge of keeping things organized. Also, folder- and

file-naming standards should be chosen early. It's critical that everyone on the committee be able to navigate whatever online tool is selected and agree to share everything through that platform. Whatever method you choose, take the time to make sure someone on the committee is skilled at navigating it. Then spend some time with the committee training everyone how to access, upload, name, share, and save documents. If your file creation, file-naming, and folder-naming conventions and software-sharing procedures are well organized and easy for everyone to access and use, your work will be much easier.

In our case, tasks were handled by whoever had the expertise and the time. In some cases, we were fortunate to have staff members that we could turn to for help. Our committee members were so dedicated that there was always someone willing to step up and do whatever needed to be done. Now that we have two years under our belts, it's easy to see that assigning specific tasks to specific people would be far more efficient.

Decisions, Decisions

Assuming that you are thinking about launching your own version of the STBF Author Project, this book and our experience can help make your initial project a little easier. You can easily put your own state, district, or county name into the STBF name. That was, in fact, one of the things we had in mind when we chose the name.

We also thought about the current culture, what was popular, the buzzwords we were hearing. We were also thinking about the reality shows that were popular at the time and the whole competition angle. Reality show competitions were very hot: *Dancing with the Stars, American Idol, Survivor*, etc. Our notes from a meeting on July 9, 2013, read: "We need to hold an *America's Got Talent* for Illinois authors (*Illinois's Got Authors* ???—we need to come up with a catchy title for what we are doing!)."

Here are some of the names we considered:

- Ultimate Author Challenge
- Indie Author Challenge
- The Best Prairie State Author You're Not Reading
- The Unknown Illinois Author of the Year
- The Soon to be Famous Illinois Author of the Year

We knew we needed "author" and "Illinois" in the name. Again, our marketing experience guided our decision. We knew it couldn't be too long, hard to say, or hard to remember. Even at that time, we were thinking we wanted a model that other people, other states, could replicate.

Eventually we settled on "The Soon to be Famous Illinois Author Project." We knew that was a little long, but it was doable. It could easily be adapted for

Figure 2.1. The Soon to be Famous Illinois Author Project logo, created by Theresa Papaurelis.

other states. We quickly started using the shortened Soon to be Famous among ourselves and started thinking about a logo.

Theresa Papaurelis, staff artist at the Indian Prairie Public Library District, turned this logo around in record-breaking time. Her vision was of an author at a typewriter, hence the font she chose, and a quickly added proofreader's mark inserting the phrase "soon to be famous." We loved it! It emphasized our main ideas—Illinois and author—while creatively adding "soon to be famous." We have since trademarked the name and logo. (See figure 2.1.)

We envisioned how it would look on a Web site, in print, and on Facebook. We liked it: The Soon to be Famous Illinois Author Project.

Like most things for this project, our name was a result of quick thinkers, speedy brainstorming, and a looming deadline. Many of the decisions that we made putting this project together were spurred on by impending deadlines—which is an approach I highly recommend. If you've ever been subjected to months of committee meetings to arrive at decisions by consensus—or no decision at all—you'll understand why. We put our heads together, kicked ideas around, and came to our own consensus/decision in a record-breaking amount of time.

Once your committee is in place, there are still many decisions to be made before you can announce the project. All the details about author submissions and judging have to be in place so that you can create a process for submissions, forms for judge applications, scoring rubrics for entries, etc. Here are some particulars you will have to consider:

- Define the genres you want to judge.
- Decide on the formats you will accept.
- Anticipate the questions that an author might ask.
- Design your submission form (or use ours); do some usability testing if you can. Ask someone to try to complete the submission form to see if it's easy to use and if it actually garners all the information you need.

We started with the broadest parameters in establishing submission guidelines. We knew we wanted Illinois authors who were self-published; they had to be authors currently living in Illinois, not just born in Illinois, a previous resident of Illinois, or an author who wrote about things/people/places in Illinois.

We considered genres and age categories and decided that adult fiction was a broad enough category that we would get submissions, while it was inclusive enough to encompass genres such as mysteries, romance, science fiction, and fantasy. As long as it was fiction intended for adults, it would qualify.

Next we considered formats. We decided to accept either print or electronic copies. As with most other things with this project, we figured it out as we went along. And in fact, we decided in year two that electronic submissions were a must.

Notes from a meeting we had on September 16, 2013, show that we had just decided on all these parameters less than a month before the ILA conference in October. We were moving at a breakneck pace at this point: securing free booth space at ILA and designing banners, posters, bookmarks, flyers, nomination forms, judges' applications, and the Web site.

How involved will you want libraries and librarians to be? We really wanted librarians to be involved and invested, to serve as judges, and we started out thinking that librarians would actually read and recommend books for the competition. Ultimately, as the project progressed and questions began coming in, we realized that many librarians felt they didn't have the time to read and recommend a self-published book. Some felt that the quality of self-published books was, in general, inferior; some felt that they weren't comfortable passing judgment or weren't qualified to "recommend" a self-published book. And buzz about the project hadn't really spread outside of the marketing arena, so many librarians were not familiar with the project. We rethought this part of the project and realized that, by asking librarians to make the initial recommendations for the books, we were using them as the first line of judging, and that really was not our intention.

We actually tweaked this part of the process while we were accepting submissions in the first year of the project by asking that the nominations be funneled through a library, creating a connection among the author, the library, and the competition. We felt that this would encourage some interest on the individual library level without unduly burdening librarians who hadn't volunteered to be judges.

Another important decision to make is to determine who your audience is and the best time and place to reach them; take an inventory of meetings, events, conventions, and campaigns that you might use to maximize your exposure. If you can target a statewide event that would make a good platform for announcing your project or for announcing the winner, you can use that date to determine deadlines and timelines for everything else: the length of time you will have to promote the project, seek author contributions, judge entries, inform libraries about how they can participate, and promote the winning author.

As the Illinois project started to come together in July 2013, we locked onto the idea of announcing the competition at the ILA annual convention in October 2013. Our audience was Illinois librarians. What better place to reach out to Illinois librarians than their annual convention, where we knew there would be hundreds of librarians who recommend books to patrons every single day; select the books that their libraries are going to purchase; read day and night and can write critiques as quickly as they can write a grocery list; and can recognize a good work of fiction from a mile away. This was our audience: librarians who would be attending the ILA convention in just three months.

We couldn't envision another vehicle for announcing the project, and we didn't want to wait for more than a year to announce it at the next year's ILA convention. We felt that the opportunity to announce at ILA was so perfect that we were willing to push ourselves to be ready. We were already thinking that National Library Week, in April 2014, would be ideal for announcing the winner. As marketers, we recognized the value that the additional support of a statewide convention and a national event such as National Library Week could have for the project.

PARTNERSHIPS

Partnerships can help you reach your goals for your author project. Research organizations and determine whether their mission aligns with your project. In forming partnerships with other organizations, it's necessary to spell out what each partner can contribute.

As you form your partnerships, look to every organization and networking group on the local, statewide, and regional stages for buy-in and partners. Every little bit matters. Determine what your partners can offer to the project, such as

- cross publicity;
- staff members who can contribute to the graphics and the Web site;
- financial support for some of the printed materials and other promotional items;
- free booth space at conventions;
- free ad space in a magazine; or
- a platform from which you can spread the word, publish updates, and make announcements.

The STBF committee sought out partners wherever we could: district meetings; networking groups; readers' advisory groups; and Heartland and RAILS, our two Illinois library systems.

Because of the partnership we had with ILA, we were able to get booth space at their 2013 annual convention at no charge to promote the project. Because the subject of eBook pricing was on everyone's minds, RAILS was already planning a workshop about eBooks at the ILA convention, and they generously allowed us to announce our project.

After making our announcement, we rushed to our booth at the exhibit hall. We were able to talk one on one with librarians who stopped at the booth; we started signing up judges on the spot. The Public Library Association (PLA) and Illinois Heartland Library System (the library system for southern

Illinois) were also at the convention, so we were able to tell them about the project. Our list of partners was growing.

In the initial STBF project, it was clearly to our advantage to put the names of our partners on our printed materials and Web site, and our project was publicized through their networks. These partnerships also added legitimacy to this project.

PROMOTION

Once you have settled on an announcement date, the pressure starts to build. This type of project means you are actually reaching out to two different audiences: librarians and authors. At the same time that you are encouraging authors to submit their self-published books, you are trying to inform librarians about the project, get them excited, and encourage them to nominate authors. Remember to target your materials, press releases, flyers, and social media updates to the right audience.

Along with traditional promotional tools such as press releases and social media, reach out to professional organizations, networking groups, writers' workshops, and even independent bookstores. Research where budding writers gather for support and encouragement; libraries often host writers' groups. Tap into any groups for readers' advisors, book selectors, and reviewers. Reach out to every contact you have to find avenues for publicity. Enlist every person on your committee to do the same; create a contact list based on all these sources. Include professional publications and blogs as you build your contact list.

Send out press releases announcing the project, the support of another group, and the approaching deadlines. Share that information via your Web site and social media with networking and professional groups.

Creating a Web site to consolidate the details about your project is critical. Printed materials aren't always convenient or practical. With a Web presence, you will find yourself continually directing people to go to the site. Once all your contest parameters are in place, get them online. Through our Web site, we were able to archive our press releases, share our photos, link to media coverage, and keep our audience updated.

DESIGNING A WEB SITE FOR AN AUTHOR AWARDS PROJECT
Jennifer Amling

An eye-catching, well-designed Web site can attract people to your author award project and encourage them to get involved, whether they are authors, librarians, library directors, or even prospective sponsors. It is an inexpensive way to explain the project's history, objectives, and accolades; identify the organizers; put the spotlight on the winning authors and sponsoring libraries as well as supporters of the project; and provide information to those who yearn to be famous authors! I began working on the soontobefamous.info site in its second year. Although the site offered up quite a bit of information, I wanted to do a redesign to freshen up the look, feel, and content.

It is important to keep updating your author award Web site to keep it "fresh" and inviting. Using popular colors in the design, as well as posting photos of people involved in the project, can be effective. A Web site with long-running text and few graphics will not encourage viewers to stay interested in your project. Videos on your Web site, especially something humorous, will also keep people tuned in. A Facebook video post I created with the STBF contest information reached 275 people with 18 shares in three days. If each of those 18 people shared it with another 18 people, the reach could go on and on!

We used several pictures of our winner from last year's contest; a video made by the Soon to be Famous team showing the ease of how to enter; as well as several large, colored links directing our visitors to easy-to-follow instructions.

You might include links like "I'm a librarian, what should I do?" and "I'm an author, what should I do?" Also useful are "How to Make an .EPUB file" and "How to publish your book on Smashwords."

We updated our site every time our first winner, Joanne Zienty, did something new or interesting. We updated her calendar of events, her book sales figures, and pictures of her at speaking engagements. We also tried to update deadlines and ways to upload the documents. We added logos of our sponsors and links to become a part of the judging process.

Make sure you back up your site every time you make a change. You don't want to lose all your new content if your server crashes! Once you have your visitors engaged, be prepared to receive a high volume of questions and comments from prospective entrants. I constantly had to check the site to see if anyone had asked questions or sought help, especially as the deadline approached. You'll want to assign this task to someone who knows the workings of the contest inside and out. Because I was new to the group and was answering almost all the questions, I often had to find the answer from another member of our STBF committee. This caused a delay in responding to authors' questions, which is something you want to avoid.

The success of your Web site can depend on how easily it can be found. Proper design, such as the correct coding, will pave the way. If you are not familiar with how to do this, there are several tutorials available on YouTube or just by searching with Google. I highly recommend using a WordPress site, as I feel it has only a mild learning curve and could easily be put together by a novice Web site designer. WordPress also offers plug-ins for your code that allow you to create slideshows, application forms, image links, or almost anything else you might need. Our site could be accessed through a direct link from Facebook or our RAILS site, or by typing the URL into a browser from a brochure or flyer. Make sure your URL is easy to remember and to the point, so your users can easily type it into their browsers. Our URL, soontobefamous.info, is relatively easy to remember, but you may want to use something even shorter and easier to remember, like famousauthor.info or stbf.info. You can check to see if the URL you want to use is available on a variety of sites, such as availableurl.net.

Before your Web site goes live, have someone test it to ensure navigation is easy and fast. Requiring each author to upload his or her application and book individually can lead to a lot of technical errors. About 75 percent of our authors/librarians had no problems uploading content. The other 25 percent did have some issues. In all likelihood, this was not a result of technical errors with the site. However, that 25 percent was cause for concern, leading us to question the usability of our site. If 25 percent of the authors who want to enter your contest are unable to do so, that is a big problem. Our site allowed for uploads directly onto our WordPress application. An email was then sent to me as the Webmaster with the application and the book in either .EPUB or .MOBI format. This was originally set up as the default, since I was doing the redesign of the site. I recommend instead setting up an email address that will accept all applications and forward them to all committee members. There was a fair amount of manually forwarding emailed applications, which is a little dangerous lest some applications get lost in the shuffle.

You may want to consider making the application form available to download in Word format, which can then be filled out and attached to an email. Google Forms would also be an effective method. Hopefully all your prospective entrants can attach files to an email, but some authors may need help from their friendly neighborhood librarian. The simpler the process, the more prospective authors your contest will attract.

The Web site is just one tool that you should be using to get your message out to the masses. Our audience consisted entirely of self-published authors who lived in the state of Illinois.

In summary, keep your content fresh, clean, and easily navigable. Hire a Web designer if you need to; even a student could get the job done if you know what you want. Make a plan and be sure to promote your Web page at every available opportunity.

Remember word-of-mouth marketing. Talk about your project everywhere you go and to whomever will listen. In one of the most random, quirky series of events, a casual conversation that I had with a library patron led to a lengthy article about the project in the *Chicago Tribune* on New Year's Day, 2014, just five days before the author submission deadline of January 6. Before that article appeared, we were thrilled to have 40 submissions, well beyond our initial goal of 25. Another 60 authors submitted books after this article appeared, stretching our already stressed and overworked committee to respond. We extended the deadline when this deluge of submissions coincided with a brutal (even for Chicago) Polar Vortex that stranded travelers and closed libraries.

Dare I Say It? Think Outside the Box

Today, if you have a smartphone, you can make a video. Shoot a quick message about the project; find an author who is excited about the project; talk to a librarian who supports the project; or create a parody of the Oscars. Put as much time and effort into it as you can. Start a YouTube channel for your project and post frequent short videos; share them on Facebook and Twitter. Tie into whatever is trending.

Somewhere along the line, we started talking about shooting a promotional video to publicize the project. Since we were approaching the holidays, *It's A Writingful Life* was conceived—a parody of the holiday classic *It's A Wonderful Life.* The script featured Georgette Bailey, a writer struggling with writer's block who hastily wishes that books never existed. Angel Claire grants her wish, allowing both of them a glimpse into an unfriendly world where books do not exist. Will Georgette find new inspiration to finish her writing and submit her book to the Soon to be Famous Illinois Author Project?

In yet another hard-to-believe confluence of events, both Dee Brennan, executive director of RAILS, and Bob Doyle, executive director of ILA, were available and agreed to be part of the video shoot. A host of library directors created funny photos of themselves in a world without books. We gathered on the Wednesday before Thanksgiving to begin shooting.

In what would soon turn out to be a trend for our project, the day was bitterly cold, though clear and sunny. Everyone who had agreed to pitch in on this project showed up. We were handed scripts; parts were assigned; and within about two hours, the video was shot, brilliantly directed by Karen McBride of the Barrington Public Library. We created a coffee shop in the library's cafe and shot scenes outside the library, at the desk, in the stairwell, in front of a Christmas tree, and outdoors at a nearby lake.

The creativity of our group was amazing—almost as amazing as everyone's continued willingness to jump in and do whatever needed to be done. Many of us saw the script for the first time that day and took on small parts as needed. The staff at Indian Prairie Public Library was phenomenal, stopping in the middle of their workday to act as patrons in the coffee shop, reporters, and even Bert and Ernie (not the Sesame Street version!). We laughed, we shivered, and we patted ourselves on the back.

TIMELINE FOR THE SOON TO BE FAMOUS !LLINOIS AUTHOR PROJECT

2013	Soon to be Famous Illinois Author Project Timeline
June 28	David Vinjamuri speaks at ALA
July 5	Met with RAILS
July 9	Presented Idea to RAILS Marketing Group
July 26	Presented Idea to ILA Marketing Committee and annual orientation meeting
Sept. 16	General parameters for competition are determined
Oct. 8	Booth Secured at ILA Conference 2013
Oct. 14	Promotional materials ready
Oct. 15–17	Project announced at ILA
Nov. 8	First press release sent out
Nov. 26	Video produced
Dec. 4	Video released
Dec. 31	40 submissions
Jan. 1, 2014	Chicago Tribune article published
Jan. 6	Original deadline—additional 60 entries received
Jan. 7	Polar Vortex hits Chicago

WHAT WE LEARNED

Our committee was never formalized. There was no chairman, no subcommittees, no mission statement. What we lacked in organizational structure, we made up for in excitement, creativity, and networking.

We all managed to contribute to this within the parameters of our daily work lives (and beyond). We volunteered, collaborated, produced, wrote, promoted, photographed, and networked. It was an incredible experience, culminating in a very successful first and second year of seeking self-published authors. We learned more about self-publishing than we could have imagined. We started out to do something about the outrageous pricing policies that libraries faced, and we learned that there is a whole world of self-published books that librarians must learn to navigate to bring the best materials to readers.

We learned from our experience. One of the key changes we incorporated in our second year was defining specific tasks for specific people. If we wanted this project to live beyond its first year, we knew we couldn't depend on everyone to keep working at the pace they had during the inaugural year. We broke down the various jobs into manageable, time-limited tasks. Once we had those in hand, we were lucky to find a few new, fabulous volunteers to keep the committee going. We learned that our passion for this project lit a fire under all of us.

REFERENCE

Vinjamuri, D. (2013). The $84 question: Why libraries matter and can do more in the era of e-books, social media and branding. PR Forum 2013, American Library Association Annual Conference, Chicago, IL.

3

GETTING OTHERS INVOLVED IN THE PROJECT

Denise Raleigh

Launching an author awards project can use many forms of emerging technology: ePublishing, communicating via the Web, electronic forms, and more. The Soon to be Famous Illinois Author project did just this. But please make no mistake, this project is about people. It uses wonderful library professionals as crowd source collection developers and marketers.

This is a perfect project to make its mark on the library history continuum, as libraries are based on an original lending model of people working together. Thousands of years ago it was about everybody sharing a handwritten scroll. Now there is a huge need for people to work together to handle the people- and machine-created scrolls that are being produced faster than anyone could ever have imagined. If the number of self-published books keeps rising at this incredible rate, this project will seem more like the SETI (Search for Extraterrestrial Intelligence) among the stars.

GETTING SPONSORS AND BACKING

At the time of this writing, everyone in the book world—librarians, publishers, and authors—sees the proverbial elephant in the corner. Self-publishing is here, growing exponentially, and we need to be able to determine the jewels that are among these titles. Therefore, finding supporters for a project that encourages library professionals to assist in culling titles to find good reads shouldn't be difficult. In our case, it took Dee Brennan, the executive director of the Reaching Across Illinois Library System (RAILS), about one minute to decide to support the project after we described it to her. Bob Doyle, the executive director of the Illinois Library Association (ILA), was equally as fast and decisive about backing Soon to be Famous.

After RAILS and ILA were on board, the American Library Association's Digital Content Working Group, the Public Library Association, the Illinois Heartland Library Association, and the Chicago Public Library signed on as supporters, helping to get the word out to other libraries and authors.

"Libraries and librarians are experts at recognizing exceptional literature and promoting the works of authors. We are just taking this role a step further and transforming it into an exciting project for writers and libraries," said Dee Brennan, Executive Director of RAILS (Reaching Across Illinois Library System) (STBF Project, 2013; see figure 3.1).

Figure 3.1. Dee Brennan.

"IHLS is pleased to partner with a project that connects libraries to the communities they serve. It's a perfect match—libraries seek out and promote literary resources, and patrons look to them to offer engaging and enticing options. Imagine discovering the latest literary genius in your backyard!" added Leslie Bednar, Executive Director of the Illinois Heartland Library System (STBF Project, 2013; see figure 3.2).

Figure 3.2. Leslie Bednar.

Figure 3.3. Bob Doyle.

"David (talking about David Vinjamuri) made the point again and again about how libraries are instrumental in promoting reading and literature. He issued a challenge to libraries to find an unknown talented Illinois author that will become a success based on librarians' recommendations. So we are taking up the challenge! The purpose of this exciting project is twofold—give a talented author exposure and spotlight the importance of libraries to literature efforts," Illinois Library Association Executive Director Robert Doyle (STBF Project, 2013; see figure 3.3).

Figure 3.4. Larra Clark.

"This project fits well with the ALA Digital Content Working Group's efforts to step up engagement with authors, publishers and others in the eBook ecosystem to ensure readers have access to literature and knowledge in all formats through libraries," said Larra Clark, Deputy Director of ALA Office for Information Technology Policy. "Self-publishing is exploding, so the Soon to be Famous Illinois Author project comes at a great time to benefit readers and writers across the state. I can imagine many other states taking up the challenge, and I hope they will." (STBF Project, 2013; see figure 3.4).

PLA president and Illinois librarian Carolyn Anthony stated that, "Public libraries have a real role to play in encouraging local authors, helping them learn about options for self-publishing, giving their works visibility in the library, and spreading the word when a rising star emerges. PLA is delighted to support this effort and looks forward to helping to build on this wonderful idea!" (STBF Project, 2013; see figure 3.5).

Figure 3.5. Carolyn Anthony.

The other element that makes this project near and dear to supporters is its cost. It can be done well on a small budget. Our budget for the first year of this project was $250 from ILA to pay for a well-designed Web site at www. soontobefamous.info (see figure 3.6) and $125 from RAILS (see figure 3.7) for bookmarks to give away at the annual Illinois Library Association conference. In-kind donations were also extremely valuable. ILA provided free

Figure 3.6. The Illinois Library Association contributed $250 for the STBF Web site.

Figure 3.7. RAILS contributed $125 for the STBF bookmarks.

booth space at the conference (see figure 3.8), and it was exhilarating to be empowered to reach out to everyone walking by to explain the project. It gave us a new appreciation of the many types of people who work in the Illinois library ecosystem.

Enlist one of your participating libraries to provide meeting space and server space for a Web site. For example, with our group, Gail Borden Public Library provides server space for the site and support for group email lists. Eisenhower Public Library District provided a central location with a fabulous coffee shop where we could meet.

People and communities who move forward on this project will find that there are visionary library directors. You can effectively market this project using channels that you are probably already using: social media, eNewsletters,

Figure 3.8. First sign-up at the 2013 Illinois Library Association conference with Julie Stam at the booth.

and the press. You will likely find, as we did, that reporters are quite aware of the viral growth of self-publishing and were supportive of library endeavors to find the stars among the galaxies of newly self-published books.

RECRUITING JUDGES

Recruit librarians in your area to serve as judges; this highlights the experience of librarians and raises the library's profile in the community. There are many channels you can use to entice these professionals:

- Start simply by talking to librarians in your own buildings, especially concentrating on those who perform readers' advisory duties.
- Reach out to librarian readers' advisory groups.
- If your project is statewide, reach out to all the professional organizations with an eNewsletter and a Web site to carry your call-to-action message. (See figures 3.9 and 3.10.)
- Speak at any of the networking groups and conferences that will have you. (See figure 3.11.)
- Reach out to the press. In our case, the *Chicago Tribune*, the *Daily Herald*, and local community papers found this story intriguing. David Vinjamuri wrote about the project twice in his *Forbes* columns.
- Try to think through all the processes; but for the first year, be willing to accept that there will be questions you have to decide on as they arise.
- Make sure that individuals who participate have a manageable workload commitment. And make sure that they understand what you are asking of them.

GETTING LIBRARY BUY-IN

As in all walks of life, there are all kinds of people—some love to get involved with something new, some want additional information, and some are wary of the new. The given is that everyone is busy. So your first hurdle is to convince others that the project is worthwhile. Having David Vinjamuri's eye-popping numbers about the growth of self-publishing made all the difference for the Illinois Soon to be Famous Author Project. Having eBook prices going through the roof also made many people want to join; this is something you can point out to those you wish to recruit. It was also helpful that so many library leaders and organizations were tremendously supportive. We found that as our project moved along, library directors who had initially thought that they did not have staff time to participate changed their minds when they learned more.

Fun

Fun is another essential element. Try to identify a piece of the project that will bring everyone into the fun. For us, this was the idea of producing *It's a*

SOON TO BE FAMOUS ILLINOIS AUTHORS PROJECT

Illinois libraries hope to discover an unknown author whose work will jump off the page for readers.

Illinois Author Project

The *Soon to be Famous Illinois Author* project will be accepting **adult fiction** submissions from Illinois residents via their local libraries. The *Soon to be Famous Illinois Author* will be announced during National Library Week, April 13 to 19, 2014.

It is the perfect fit for Illinois libraries to discover an exciting work of fiction, as libraries have been a keystone in creating enthusiasm for reading for centuries. Even in this digital age, every day, library staff recommend written works as well as host author talks and book clubs.

The *Soon to be Famous Illinois Author* project was inspired by a presentation by brand expert and NYU professor David Vinjamuri, who spoke about the importance of libraries in the era of eBooks and branding at the American Library Association's annual conference last summer.

Authors, please submit your great story to your local library (public, school, academic, special), before January 6th.

At the ILA's 2013 Annual Conference, project information will be part of the Tuesday, October 15, 1:45 p.m. program *E-book Essentials: Everything You Need to Know about E-books and Libraries Now.* Also, stop by Booth 131, the project's information booth. For more information, <u>please click</u> here.

Figure 3.9. The Illinois Library Association eNewsletter.

Writingful Life, a parody of the film *It's a Wonderful Life*. The concept was to show the awful prospects in a community when a writer decides not to write. (See figure 3.12.)

You will likely find, as we did, that there are many talented people who are willing to get involved. Karen McBride is a supremely talented videographer, and Liz Clemmons is a wonderful writer. Veronda Pitchford delivered an Academy Award–worthy performance for us in the role of Georgette, and Nikki Zimmermann was born to play the angel. This video

Figure 3.10. The Illinois Heartland Library System Web site.

Figure 3.11. Julie Stam and Denise Raleigh do some impromptu marketing at the Illinois Library Association Conference.

Figure 3.12. *It's a Writingful Life* can be viewed at http://bit.ly/writingfullife.

opened the virtual door for participation from across the state, as there was a scene in which ILA's Bob Doyle showed Georgette the many people who fought to save the books. This snippet in the video was an opportunity to get many more people involved. As you can see, there were a number of Illinois library directors who joined the fun by emailing photos. You needn't create a video if that seems too intimidating, but try to find something that will engage participants in a fun and meaningful way. To create attention, inclusion, and sharing, fun is the key. There are numerous ways to engage. Many of the northern Illinois marketing professionals met to learn more about social media in 2014. During the discussion, everyone seemed to be experiencing the same engagement reactions to different posts: people engaged much more with pictures of people coming to work wearing the same outfits than with serious event posts.

Heartland's Leslie Bednar sent a photo, as did a number of library directors. Carole Medal of Gail Borden created a demo poster so that everyone else would know what we were looking for. Figure 3.13 shows the poster of various directors in Illinois who lent a hand with this promo.

Figure 3.13. Several Illinois library directors generously agreed to have a poster made of them saving books for the committee to use in *It's a Writingful Life*.

Word to the wise—do not shoot in subzero weather as non-frostbite wardrobe is hard. (See figures 3.14 and 3.15.)

Figure 3.14. Videographer Laura Espinoza and filming coordinator Cris Cigler were good sports as the frostbite set in during filming of *It's a Writingful Life*.

Figure 3.15. Director Karen McBride fished the script out of the frozen creek after "Georgette" threw her book away.

Communication

Assumptions are the termites of relationships.
—Henry Winkler

As you know, communication is good not only for the Fonz, but for everyone else as well. Throughout your project, keep people in the loop on a continual basis, letting supporters know that their support is warranted and that taking the time to participate is worthwhile. Update through email, Facebook, the Web site, and Flickr photos—this was fundamental to keeping the Soon to be Famous message alive. We even used YouTube to live stream the Soon to be Famous award ceremony during National Library Week in 2013.

Be committed to continually listening. Make changes based on participants' thoughts when it makes sense and answer questions as quickly as you can. Be open to crowd sourcing the process as well as the contest. What you will find in getting others involved is that your community members are smart and fun. And you are going to make some great new friends. (See figures 3.16 and 3.17.)

Figure 3.16. The Soon to be Famous committee members in year one. Left to right: Sue Wilsey of Niles Public Library, Julie Stam of Eisenhower Public Library District, Liz Clemmons of Gail Borden Public Library, Cris Cigler of Indian Prairie Public Library, Anita Quinlan of Plainfield Public Library, Denise Raleigh of Gail Borden Public Library, Nicole Zimmermann of La Grange Public Library and Donna Fletcher of Donna E. Fletcher Consulting, Inc. and the Highland Park Public Library Board.

Figure 3.17. Joining in year two were Lucy Tarabour of Clarendon Hills Public Library and Jennifer Amling of Helen Plum Memorial Library. Left to right: Cris Cigler, Denise Raleigh, Lucy Tarabour, Donna Fletcher, Anita Quinlan, Sue Wilsey, Julie Stam, Jennifer Amling, and Nicole Zimmermann.

REFERENCE

STBF Author Project. (2013, October 30). Undiscovered author needed by Illinois libraries to become famous. Retrieved from http://soontobefamous.info/press-release/

4

COMMUNICATING WITH AUTHORS, ACCEPTING SUBMISSIONS, AND THE POLAR VORTEX

Donna Fletcher

TIME FOR NOMINATIONS

Once the publicity and buzz start, you'll hear from authors wanting to get their books nominated. So be sure to create a nomination form before you publicize the contest. It can be a paper or an online document. Here are some things to consider when you develop the nomination form.

One way is to create a Word document, which requires no special technology or coding skills. You can put it on the project's Web site and ask the nominators to send the completed nomination form to the project's email or other designated address. If the nominees typed in the information, they can simply attach the Word file. Others may want to submit a handwritten document. In that case, it has to be scanned and then emailed.

However, consider how many pages may be needed for the paper questionnaire. It may be several pages long, which you have to print and file. If you receive a lot of completed nominations, it gets a bit more difficult to track and file all of them. (The STBF Project received 103 nominations in its first year!)

For the first year, we posted a Word document on the STBF Web site that required the sponsoring library and author to complete the form together. Once it was finished, the author or sponsoring librarian emailed it to the STBF address. After it was received, the committee contacted the author to send copies of the book.

Another option is an online application, which we tried in the second year. Both the author and sponsoring library had specific sections to complete in the nominating form. However, the online application didn't allow anyone to save his or her nomination. This caused both the librarian and author to send separate nomination forms—the author provided his information and the librarian her information. These two documents sometimes arrived weeks apart, making it difficult to pair the author with the sponsoring library. Some authors encountered difficulty uploading the application, which was addressed by posting a Word nomination form on the STBF Web site. For the future, we intend to continue with an online application that can be saved as the nomination is developed.

TRACKING THE NOMINATIONS

It's important to track the nominations to know who is submitting and ensure that the application is complete with contact information. It's a good idea to appoint an author coordinator who will review all of the nominations and can keep the committee up-to-date on the number of nominations and which libraries are participating. In our case, once we verified that all of the requested information was complete, we assigned a number for the nomination and entered the information into an Excel spreadsheet. Following are some of the columns we used:

- Nomination number
- Author last name
- Author first name
- Book title
- Author email address
- Author phone number
- Author physical address
- Sponsoring library
- Library nominator
- Library nominator phone number, email
- Library director
- Digital file link

GETTING THE BOOKS TO THE JUDGES

Another consideration is determining how the author will send the nominated book: with the nomination or separately? Also, do you want the authors to submit paper books or eBooks? In our experience, most of the authors had both types. As you decide which books to request, think about where your judges reside. If they are scattered around your state, it's probably best to request eBook formats. That way the judge coordinator can easily disseminate the books to the judges. If your committee prefers printed books, then you will need to find ways to mail the books to the judges or have judges come to pick up the books at one of the participating libraries or consortiums. In the second year of the STBF Project, the nomination form required each author to attach a .MOBI or .EPUB digital file or a link to a digital file on Amazon, Barnes & Noble, or Smash-words. Almost all of the authors could readily send the requested files, and it was a far more efficient way to send the digital files to the judges.

SENSATIONAL PR EFFECT

A well-written press release and cultivating the local media can have a huge effect on the interest in and nominations for the project. Also, your com-mittee should think about how to handle receiving a plethora of nominations days before the deadline. Here's what we encountered and handled. Just a few days before the submission deadline for nominations, a story about the STBF Project ran in the first section of the *Chicago Tribune* on New Year's Day. Suddenly, our 40 nominations swelled to 103 in less than a week, with the deadline for nominations just a few days away. To get all of these nominations submitted required that we become more flexible to help the authors with their nominations—especially because the horrendous winter weather arrived just as this article appeared. Be prepared for things that just happen and can't be planned for. Weather is one of these.

THINGS THAT HAPPEN

Weather can have a huge effect on nominations, especially if it requires both the author and a librarian to complete the nomination. Just after the *Chicago Tribune* article appeared, the Polar Vortex arrived in Illinois, causing subzero temperatures, strong winds, and drifting snow. Many businesses, schools, and libraries closed for several days. Authors quickly contacted the committee and asked if the deadline could be extended. We immediately agreed and gave authors and libraries another week to submit the nominations. The article and the later deadline led to a deluge of additional nominations, resulting in a total of 76 libraries nominating 103 books.

Many of the authors couldn't travel to their local libraries. Others visited and learned that the person who could nominate an author was absent due to snow or sickness. However, many persisted. One was Joanne Zienty, who ulti-mately was awarded the 2014 STBF honor for her book *The Things We Save*.

Here's how she completed her nomination:

Yes, I am nominating my own book due to the following circumstances: I only discovered this contest the other day through the article in the Chi-cago Tribune. If it was promoted in the email newsletters that I receive from the Illinois Library Association, I must have missed it. I started a job in a new school district this past August and that, plus taking classes, has been pretty time- and mind-consuming. When I went to my local library

(Wheaton—which, as noted above, has a copy on its shelves) on Friday to ask a staff member to submit it, I was told the person who was handling this was off sick and would not be back to work until Monday (1/6). Given that my school district is back in session on Monday and the deadline for submission is also Monday, it seemed that time was working against me. I considered calling up a few friends and acquaintances, but I thought, hey, I'm a librarian—and I have the chutzpah—and the strong belief in the quality of my book and the underlying ideals of the contest—to submit it myself. However, if you would like independent corroboration of its quality, I include the following [contact information]. (Zeinty, 2014)

SUBMITTING LIBRARIES

It's likely that you'll encounter two types of libraries as you market this project. The first is very supportive. These libraries see the value of the project: to promote, enhance, and reinforce the role of libraries to publishers. You'll probably receive many questions from interested librarians. Following are some questions you are likely to be asked, and suggested responses, so that you can formulate your own answers ahead of time.

Q: May an individual library sponsor/nominate more than one author?
This is a decision for your committee. We allowed libraries to sponsor as many authors as they wanted (in part because we had no idea how many nominations we would receive the first year). However, we asked that each author enter only one book.

Q: Can an author be nominated if he or she does not live in the library's service area?
This, too, is for your committee to decide. We allowed authors living anywhere in our state, Illinois, to be nominated. However, if you are in a less populous state, you might consider nominations from other nearby states.

Q: What about submitting nonfiction and children's books?
We suggest sticking to one type of genre for at least the first year, which for us was adult fiction. However, you could consider children's fiction or other genres.

Q: Can only public libraries submit nominations?
It's up to your committee. We allowed any type of library in the state to nominate a self-published book.

Q: Can the author send the book in a Word or PDF file on a flash drive?
We did not support these types of files because they are very difficult to read in eReader devices. We required eBook formats and online availability.

Q: The author has a digital file, but has not self-published a book. Can she be part of the project?
If your project is focused on self-publishing, then the author should submit a self-published book.

Authors also contacted us with an array of questions. Here are some for you to think about so that you can be prepared with an answer:

Q: Can an author submit a book with a collection of short stories or a graphic novel?
We decided that both would be acceptable as long as they fall into the adult fiction category. However, your committee may think differently.

Q: If the book is classified as young adult, is it eligible for the competition?
There's a fine line here. One way to handle this is to classify the novel as adult fiction on the application and let the judges decide whether or not it qualifies.

Q: Where can an author find a library that will support your STBF project?
This is an important question. We wanted to give self-published authors the opportunity to be part of the project. So for authors who could not find a supportive library, our committee helped them find a library interested in the project.

Q: Do I have to provide my address on the nomination form?
We believe it's very important to have all of the authors' contact information. If your committee requires that an author live in a particular service area or state, be sure the nominee provides his or her complete address.

NONSUBMITTING LIBRARIES

Unfortunately, there are libraries that have negative perceptions of self-published books and authors. While we all know that some self-published books are not well written or desirable in a library's collections, libraries should still consider this type of project. You will likely encounter librarians sharing their concerns about the project, which might include comments like the following:

Our library does not want to submit a nomination. The self-published authors are not accomplished and they will hurt the library's reputation.

Our staff is already overworked. They do not have time to read and vet the nominated books and complete the nomination form.

There is no reason for the library to be involved in the project.

As you might expect, authors are very miffed when the library doesn't support the project. As one author noted:

> I spoke with the person who was in charge of the branch that afternoon. She read the two pages I'd copied from the www.soontobefamous.info site describing the project and detailing how librarians could submit nominations. She dismissed the project as something that the branch had no need to participate in. She did take, though, the information I gave her about myself, my novels, and my website. She said she would give the information to the branch manager, who was not present at that time, and they would call me with their response. I've waited almost two weeks without hearing from them. ∮

WHAT THE AUTHORS WILL PROBABLY TELL YOU

Self-published authors are thrilled to participate in projects like STBF. You're likely to hear them express their gratitude for the project when they submit their nominations. They highly value libraries' support for self-published authors and see it as a natural and valuable partnership. Their compliments also help reinforce support for the project and energize the project committee and judges:

> Thank you so much for the opportunity to participate in this exciting initiative. What an awesome project! Hopefully it will be such a great success that other libraries in other states will follow suit. Our public library system is such an underutilized asset.

> What a wonderful way to show the strength of libraries—and to showcase talent as well!

> Thank-you for having such a great contest, honoring the hard work of these independent authors!

> I'm hoping that programs like this will help create a great working relationship with area authors and libraries. All of your effort and work is greatly appreciated.

> I absolutely love that you're seeking out great self-published works! I was alerted to the project by my local librarian in Palatine, who has also been tremendously supportive of local authors like myself.

REFERENCE

Zienty, Joanne. (2014). STBF nomination form.

5

JUDGING THE NOMINATED BOOKS

Julianne Stam

Much work will go into your Soon to be Famous contest before it is time to start the judging. The marketing and publicity for the contest should have been going on for months. Librarian judges should have been recruited and books submitted. Now it is time to do the work to pick a winning book. Your committee should have a contact person for the authors involved and should also have a coordinator for the judges and the judging process. The judging process can be quite involved, unlike what is shown in figure 5.1, and needs a detail-oriented person to coordinate it

Before you begin your project, think everything through carefully. Some of our challenges and oversights were deciding on/limiting submission formats for nominated books, planning the logistics of getting the books to the judges, underestimating how quickly we would need to be moving from round to round, and not realizing the necessity of teaching the professional librarian judges how to download certain types of eBooks. Hopefully what we learned along the way will help you conduct the judging process for your contest more smoothly than our first year went.

In the first year of your project, the committee may find itself dealing with unanticipated challenges and making decisions on the fly. With the experience of having run one contest under our belts, we had time to look at what worked and what didn't, so we made some changes to the process in year two. Some of the challenges we encountered, lessons we learned, and changes we have made are discussed below.

EBOOKS VERSUS PAPER BOOKS

Do you want to accept eBooks only, or both paper and eBooks? For us, submissions the first time around were in both paper and electronic format. The second year, submissions were limited to eBook formats. The inspiration for

Figure 5.1. Not the way to judge a book.

this contest was a presentation on why publishers were charging outrageous sums to libraries for eBooks, so making this a contest about self-published eBooks made sense. Limiting ourselves to eBooks in the second year made it easier for us to get the books from the authors and to the judges.

GETTING THE BOOKS TO THE JUDGES

How will you get the books to your judges? Depending on where your judges are located (ours were all over Illinois), you may wish to limit submissions to electronic formats to make distribution easier. This may not be a consideration if you are running this contest at an academic university or small library system, but if you are a member of a larger city or county system, it could make a huge difference in the ease of getting the books to the judges. The first year of the contest, we hadn't made eBooks a requirement, so we had eBooks and paper books to get to our judges. This made distribution a

File Format	Devices On Which Files Can Be Read
.EPUB	Nook, Kobo, computers with Adobe Digital Editions, tablets with the Nook App (or a variety of other eBook apps)
.MOBI / .AZW	Kindle, Kindle Fire, computers and tablets with the Kindle App
.IBOOK	Computers and tablets from Apple (no one inquired about submitting in this format)
.DOC / .DOCX / .PDF	While these could be read on most computers, these were not accepted formats for a self-published book.

Figure 5.2. Most common eBook formats.

challenge. We had 103 books in various formats to get to 23 judges. One of our goals was to recruit librarians from all over the state to serve as judges, and we succeeded—our judges were scattered across the Chicago suburbs and the state of Illinois. But then we had to figure out how to get the books to all of the judges. What we did was plan a few meetings for those able to attend. (We did not require the judges to attend meetings and communicated information mostly via email.) At these meetings we urged those judges who attended to take physical books instead of eBooks, and that worked out for us. In year two, this problem was eliminated by limiting submissions to .EPUB or Kindle .MOBI formats. (See figure 5.2.)

AVOIDING CONFLICTS OF INTEREST

Make sure your judges are objective and not biased in any way. Before any judging begins, ask them to complete a conflict of interest and confidentiality statement. (A copy of the agreement we used can be found in appendix A; you can adapt this for use in your contest.) This form basically states that judges should avoid any conflicts of interest or the appearance of conflicts of interest if they choose to participate. It also asks them to keep their participation as a judge under wraps and to keep their opinions of the books in the contest confidential until the winner is announced. Also, be sure to ask judges not to review the books on any Web site or social media outlet until after the contest is completed. If one of your judges is also a submitter of a nominated book, you may want to ask that person to not participate in the final round of judging if the book he or she submitted makes it to that round, to avoid conflicts of interest. We felt it was okay to have submitters as judges in the early rounds, when they could be assigned other books to read, and we did not encounter the situation in which one of our judges had nominated a finalist selection, but the possibility did exist, and we were fully aware of it. Being aware of the potential for conflicts of interest will ensure that your contest is above reproach.

THE JUDGING PROCESS

The nominated books should go through a number of rounds of judging, winnowing the entries down to the finalists and eventually a winner. For our contests, judging was broken into three rounds. We feel this worked very well and would recommend you try a similar structure when setting up your contest. The first round involved every book being looked at by one of our judges, who evaluated it on a variety of criteria and gave it a yes/no vote about moving it to the second round. Think of the first round as being similar to what a publisher does in going through its slush pile: your judges are doing a quick evaluation to decide if the book is worth looking at more closely. The books that made it through to the second round were read by a minimum of three judges and scored using a rubric. In the third round, the three finalists were read by all our judges and scored using the same rubric.

GETTING THE BOOKS FROM THE AUTHORS

It seems that getting books from authors should be simple, especially when you're talking about eBooks. However, this step can present challenges just as other steps do.

In the first year of the STBF project, we accepted paper books in the first round, but for the second and third rounds we only accepted eBook copies. In year two, all of the books were required to be submitted as eBook files right from the start. Authors were required to submit a copy or two for the first round, two to three copies for the second round, and an additional 18 copies for the final round, so that every one of the 23 judges had a copy for round three. If the author had access to the .MOBI (Kindle) or .EPUB file, he or she simply had to email the file to us so that we could email it to each of the judges who needed it for that round. But some authors claimed they did not have access to those files, so many needed to purchase gift copies and send them to us to send on to the judges. Sounds simple, right? It really should have been, but it wasn't. You will need to create a simple and thorough process and clearly explain it to the authors. Have printed instructions and plan to explain the process to authors more than once.

Most often when you purchase a gift eBook from Amazon, you insert the recipient's email address, and Amazon sends the book directly to that person. But if you're trying to keep the judges anonymous, this won't work. Those authors who need to purchase gift copies will have to purchase the books and have them sent to themselves, then forward them to your judge coordinator. This option is available on Amazon, but we found that it confused many of our authors. Having instructions prepared ahead of time for your author coordinator will prove to be valuable preparation. All of the authors eventually caught on, and we got all of the eBook copies we needed, but if you choose to offer this option, you can expect a little hand holding may be needed along the way.

What we learned along the way was how easy it is to deal with the books when the author has submitted the actual file. You can simply share the file with the judge who needs it in each round. By making this type of file submission mandatory in the second year of the project, we eliminated all the confusion that surrounded getting Amazon gift copies from the authors to the committee and then to the judges.

Be sure to stress to the judges that the file being shared with them is the copyrighted work of that author and should not be shared with anyone else. Since your judges will likely be professional librarians, as ours were, they should be aware of copyright laws. This was not seen as an issue by our committee, and none of the participating authors had an issue with it.

GETTING THE BOOKS TO THE JUDGES

Getting the eBooks to the judges should be an easier step in this process, right? If your judges are professional librarians who perform readers' advisory service as part of their regular duties, they should know how to find a way to read an eBook, whether it is a Kindle .MOBI file or an .EPUB file, or whether they have to redeem a gift copy from Amazon or download a free eBook from Smashwords in their chosen format. But we found that wasn't true for our judges. We were dealing with librarians from public, school, academic, and special libraries. Some were from large suburban libraries and some from small, almost rural libraries. They had a variety of skill and knowledge levels regarding eBooks. Once again, some education will likely be needed, and this can be done by email and telephone calls. You will find that the librarians you use as judges will have varying levels of experience, and you should be prepared to do some education as part of the process of coordinating the judging process. Your experience with this may differ depending on the prevalence of the use of eBooks within your library system.

There are two common versions of eBook files. An .EPUB file can be read using Adobe software on most computers. It can be read on most eReaders, except for Kindles. It usually opens quite easily on most tablets. A .MOBI file is specifically for a Kindle eReader, Kindle Fire tablet, or Kindle app on a computer or tablet. If the tablet or computer has the Kindle app, clicking on the .MOBI file will generally open it. With a Kindle eReader, the email containing the .MOBI file must be forwarded to the email address associated with the device. It would be wise to send this information to the judges along with your first-round books to make sure that they know what to do with the files they are receiving. A copy of the email that was sent to the judges with these instructions is included in appendix A. Once again, you can adapt these instructions for your use.

FIRST-ROUND JUDGING

Your judging process can begin as soon as all the nominations are received. As you acknowledge the judges' self-nominations, you may want to give them a brief outline of how your judging rounds will work and an estimated timeline for the process. When it is time for the first round to begin, again explain the judging process and rounds to the judges and distribute the criteria for the first round along with the books they will be reading and evaluating. You can think of the first round as being similar to a publisher's process of sorting a slush pile, in which the submissions are being judged on a variety of factors to see if they are worth moving on to the next step. Your judging criteria should cover a wide range of necessary fiction elements, from the presence of a plot to simple things like writing in complete sentences. Elements we had the judges look for in the first round are detailed in figure 5.3. Your criteria can differ if you are judging books for a different audience (teens or kids instead of adults) or in a specific genre that has some additional necessary elements.

Ask judges to evaluate each book according to your criteria, but consider giving them a few additional points to ponder. Could this book stand up to outside critical review? Would they recommend this book to a patron? These are very important points to think about for any library using this process, but it

---

FIRST ROUND REVIEWING – POINTS TO PONDER

Title	What does it suggest? Is it interesting?
Book Arrangement	Do the chapter breaks make sense and leave you wanting to find out what happens next?
Genre	Does the book fit expectations for its intended genre? Who is the intended audience?
Characters	Who are they? Are the characters fully realized? Can you relate to / empathize with them?
Storyline/Plot	What was the story about? Is the plot believable? Was the conclusion satisfying?
Overall	Was the book proofread and spell-checked? Does it follow common grammar rules? Did you enjoy it? Would you recommend it to someone? Who would like this book?

Will this book stand up to outside critical review?
Would you recommend this book to go to the next round of judging?
Would this book have mass appeal to a wide audience?

Figure 5.3. Reviewing guideline factors.

was even more so for our project, because David Vinjamuri had offered to do a follow-up story on our project winner only if the book chosen could stand up to outside critical review. In order to make it to the second round, the judges had to believe that the book they were judging could do this. Also, the book had to be one that the judges would recommend to a patron, exemplifying one of the goals of the project: to create a process for readers' advisory librarians to evaluate self-published books to find the best out there.

Ask your judges to decide for each book they read if they could or could not recommend it, and if they could, to decide whether it should be promoted to the second round. If they decide that more than one book should be promoted to the second round, ask them to rank those books, essentially telling you which are the best of the ones they have read.

SECOND-ROUND JUDGING

How many books will you have in your second round of judging? Our hope was that we would end up with about a dozen books in the second round, but we were unsure what the number would be since we had no way of guessing how many books would get a "yes" vote in the first round. We ended up with 15 books (out of 103) in year one and 12 books (out of 43) in year two that were given a "yes" vote to move up to the second round. We had considered those that were not first choices our "backups": if we got enough first choices, we would not include these; if we didn't get at enough, we would also include these in the second round. For your STBF Project, determine how many books would be ideal to move to the second round, but be flexible with this number in your planning process, because the number of entries and the number of judges you end up with are unpredictable.

Before giving books to the judges for scoring in the second round, have your committee investigate each one. Look at the book to make sure it is actually self-published. This may seem to be an easy thing to figure out, but in our case, it really wasn't for some books. Many books had what appeared to be a publisher listed. For some of the books, it was quite simple to figure out that they were in fact self-published when the listed publisher was the same as the author's name. Some books had to be looked at more closely because they appeared to have a publisher, but that publisher's only piece of work was the item entered into our contest. Other "publishers" can actually be paid services that authors use to produce their self-published books. We nearly disqualified one of the books that ended up being a finalist in our first year because we were unsure if the publisher listed was an actual publisher or simply the paid service that it turned out to be.

Once you make sure that all of the books in your second round are actually self-published, you need to get the books to the judges. But how many judges should read each book? Ideally, each book should go to at least three judges, but the number of books your judges will read during this round will

Soon to be Famous Illinois Author Rubric   Judge _____

How to use this rubric:
For each row, give the book a ranking from 1-12 and enter the score in the farthest right column. Total all of the individual scores. Fill in additional comments that will help with the evaluation process. Thanks!

Title					
Author					
	1 2 3	4 5 6	7 8 9	10 11 12	Score
Commercial Value	Bland with little commercial appeal	Interesting concept, but a bit of a yawner.	A pleasant read, but not a lot of thought provoking substance.	Highly enjoyable read that stimulates the intellect.	
Characterizations	Forgettable and dull.	Conventional, established characters.	Interesting, multi layered characters.	Fascinating, extremely well developed characters.	
Story telling	A challenge to get through to the end. Bored, confused.	A decent story that flows fairly well.	Story stayed with me between readings.	A page turner. Was disappointed when I finished.	
Plot	Weak introduction, tepid or disorganized development. Uninspired resolution.	Mildly interesting introduction, basic/predictable resolution.	Good introduction to set the stage; some development involving conflict, opposition or a problem; and a decent climax and resolution	Interesting introduction to set the stage; strong development involving conflict, opposition or a problem; and a riveting climax and resolution	
Accuracy and organization	Verbose writing, confusing to reader	Ideas not expressed clearly	Consistent writing	Concise and smooth writing, creative use of language	
Would you recommend to a patron?	I would not recommend	I might put on bottom of my reading list	I would add to my recommendation reading list	I would pre order a copy for them	
Total					

Additional Comments:

Figure 5.4. Rubric for Rounds Two and Three

vary based on the number of books moving on and the number of judges you have participating. We had decided to assign three judges per book as our minimum number, thinking that two people with very differing opinions could cancel out each other with a high score and a low score, but adding a third score would give a truer average rating. Using an average score in this round makes the most sense if some books have differing numbers of judges reading them.

For this round, give judges a rubric to use to calculate their scores so that all judges are basing their opinions on similar criteria. The rubric we used consisted of six sections (see figure 5.4), and judges could give up to 12 points per section for a possible total point value of 72. The six sections on our rubric were Commercial Value, Characterizations, Story Telling, Plot, Accuracy and Organization, and Would You Recommend This to a Patron? Our rubric was created by committee members with a background in education. The rubric is included in appendix A.

THIRD-ROUND JUDGING: THE FINALISTS

After calculating the average score for each book in round two, move your top three books on to the final round. You may find that at this point in the process, your committee members want some direct contact with the authors. Call authors to inform them that they are finalists, explain the last round of judging, ask if they are willing to assist in the promotion of the project and their book if they win, make sure they are available for the announcement event, and ask them to sign off on a legal document stating that they are the legal owners of the works they submitted. Once you get this document back and have enough copies of your books for each of the judges, it is time for the final round.

Before sending the final-round books to the judges, you may choose to hold conference calls between the committee and each of the finalists to outline the expectations should they win. This helps you ensure that these authors are willing and able to visit or teleconference with groups in libraries in your system. Whereas our committee fully intended to promote the winner to try to make that author "famous," we also expected the winner to play an active role in promoting the book and our contest. In both years we had fantastic authors as our finalists, but we might have needed to put a plan in place to deal with any author not as willing to be a full participant in the "making famous" part of the process. Your committee should consider these issues also.

In your final round of judging, every judge should read all three books and score them using the same rubric that was used in the second round. While we gave the judges the option to add comments in the second round on their rubric, for the third round they were instructed to write a short review to accompany their scores. You can use quotes from the reviews later in press releases and at your announcement event. (See figure 5.5.) For more information on instructing judges in book review writing, see appendix B.

There are two ways to look at the numbers of the final round. If all of your judges read all three books, a simple total of the points each book received should give you a winner. Another way to look at these numbers is to calculate an average for each book. While this would be necessary only if you had some judges who did not complete all of their reading and scoring, it gives you another way to look at the numbers. Consider and agree on which way you will judge before you get to this point so there are no misunderstandings. While we kept the scores of the books private, you may choose to use the scores received when promoting your winner.

Judging Round	# of Books	Time Period	Requirements
1st	Varies based on numbers of submissions	About one month	Judging guidelines with points to ponder Form for yes/no vote
2nd	About a dozen	One week per book given to judges	Scoring rubric
3rd	Three finalists	Three weeks	Scoring rubric

Figure 5.5. Summary of the three rounds of judging.

THE WINNING BOOK

Once the final-round scores have been added up, your committee will know the name of the winner. This is information that must be kept secret until your announcement event and should be known by as few people as possible, basically on a need-to-know basis. Our committee chose to announce the winner during National Library Week, figuring that this story would get more attention from the press that way. You will need to choose a location and date for your event midway through the process so that you can inform your finalists when they make the final round.

Our announcement events were held at our library system headquarters the first year and at the offices of our state library association the second year. Another choice for the location of the announcement could be the nominating library of the winning book. We chose not to do that because we wanted to establish the location before we began the final round of judging. Using the nominating library of the winning entry as a location necessitates having all of the libraries hold space for announcement day until you know who the winner is. Either way, when you contact the finalists to talk to them about what will be expected of the winner, let them know the location and time of the announcement event and that they would have to be present.

Send out press releases about the event to local and national publications, including *Library Journal* and *Publishers Weekly*. Our announcement event was preceded by a presentation on the state of publishing and libraries by David Vinjamuri, our inspiration for the STBF project. Many in the audience then stayed for the announcement event. Representatives from our library system and state library association spoke about why they became involved in the project. All finalists were given time to speak about their writing processes, why they chose to self-publish, and what being a part of the STBF contest meant to them. They were also asked to speak on the importance of libraries in their lives. They were introduced with snippets of the judges' comments about their books from their reviews.

When it comes time to announce the winner, having something similar to the envelopes used at the Oscars makes it seem more formal. We used a cover meant to hold a small tablet, and the cover of the winner's book mounted on foam board was inserted. This gave the presenter something to show the audience as the winner was announced. A committee member was nearby with a glass-etched award to present to the winner as he or she came up to the podium. Make sure that the winner has plenty of time to react to winning. Needless to say, this is a photo opportunity of which you should definitely take advantage.

Once you have announced your winner, your committee's work is not over. The next step in the process is to make that person "famous," and those on your committee tasked with doing the marketing and PR should be working on this from the moment the announcement event is being planned. They will also be hard at work during the event, live tweeting and taking photos. After the announcement, the process of making the winner "famous" becomes a partnership between your committee and your winner.

SNEAK PEEK AT THE SOON TO BE FAMOUS FINALISTS

In the spirit of making our authors famous, and because some readers may need convincing about the quality of self-published books, we include here a list of the 2014 and 2015 finalists, along with excerpts from our two winners.

2014 Soon to be Famous Illinois Author Finalists

Change of Address by Rick Polad (http://rickpolad.com/)
Warming Up by Mary Hutchings Reed (http://maryhutchingsreed.com/)
The Things We Save (2014 Winner) by Joanne Zienty (http://www.joannezienty.com/)

2015 Soon to be Famous Illinois Author Finalists

Wicked Waves by Sharon Kay (http://sharonkaynovels.com/)
The Commons Book 1: The Journeyman (2015 Winner) by Michael Alan Peck (http://michaelalanpeck.com/)
The House of Closed Doors by Jane Steen (http://www.janesteen.com)

Excerpt from the 2014 Winner: *The Things We Save* **by Joanne Zienty**
Copyright © 2011 Joanne E. Zienty

CHAPTER 1

Everyone has a box. Oh, don't bother to deny it. You have one, you know it. It might be an old-fashioned steamer trunk made of wood, strapped with worn leather bands and framed with embossed metal corners. It might be a hyper-feminine heart-shaped box, lined in velvet or satin, girlish in pink or flaming in scarlet. Maybe it's a banker's box with an orderly progression of beige manila file folders. Or an ornately carved Chinese box with its surprising secret of a box within a box within a box—the opening of all those lids leading to . . . what?

That depends on who you are. For just as we all have boxes, same but different, what's inside them varies with the owner. One woman's treasure is another woman's trash. My artifacts, your detritus. My talisman, your fetish. Relics, debris, mementos, sediments, keepsakes, crumbs. And maybe it's not even the things themselves that are important—but how they got there, who they belonged to, why they were saved instead of discarded, why they were put in the box.

Because that's the story, isn't it? The story where you are the hero, on your hero's journey, answering the call to adventure, encountering your mentor, crossing the threshold to the other world where you'll be tested and forge alliances and make enemies and face the ultimate ordeal. It's the story where you seize the elixir or the jewel or the ring and flee down the road, pursued by the furies, which you will vanquish. Or perhaps not. But you *will* return to your world, transformed, with the treasure in hand, older, wiser, a survivor.

And you'll place the object in your box. And set off on the next big adventure, for we are all Scheherazade, with tales to fill a thousand and one nights, warding off the sword with the cliffhanger.

At some point, you'll stop adding things to the box, thinking that particular tale is at an end. And you'll tuck it away in a closet or up in the attic or down in the basement. And you'll forget about it . . . well, not really forget. You'll just move it out of your working memory, to free up space. But then one day you'll come across it, maybe when you're spring cleaning, or gathering items to drop off at the Recycling Extravaganza, or searching for that black cape that has attired many a Halloween trick-or-treater, from Dracula to Darth Vader. And when you open the box, the present-day world will fall away, and it will be just you and the things you saved, and the story.

This is what it means to be haunted.

The call came on a Tuesday evening in early May. The lilacs on the bush outside the back door were already withering, their sweet perfume decaying into a musky, earthier odor just this side of rot, the purple blossoms bruised and wilting, melting at the touch of my hand. Through the screen door I saw Tally lunge for the telephone with the lithe grace and awkward anticipation of a sixteen year old in love. Her initial tone was low, expectant, almost sultry. Then her voice changed to the higher pitch of a child talking to an adult.

She murmured into the phone, turning every now and then to gaze over her shoulder in the direction of the screen door and me. Then she held out the receiver and said loudly, to no one in particular, "It's Grandpa Joe."

So of course Aaron had to take it. He rose from the armchair he claims as his own when he's in residence, put his journal down on the end table with a weary sigh and glanced through the window as he made his way to the telephone.

I stepped down off the patio and moved to the stone bench under the maple tree, the better to watch him through the sunporch window, to interpret the tone and import of the conversation through his body language, because when he talked to my father he never talked loud enough for me to hear, as if to punish me for the great sin of refusing to talk to him myself.

He's a big man, tall, broad-shouldered and just starting to go a little soft around the middle as he moves into his 50s. When I first met him, he was lanky, raw-boned, just starting to fill out again after his tour in Vietnam and the after-math years. Strong-jawed. That Dutch Vanderhout blood. His blonde hair was already streaked with gray then. Now it's gold and silver white. My old man.

Listening intently, the receiver pressed to his ear, his shoulders fell into a slump, as some aspect of the conversation deflated him. He sat down at the secretary and ran the fingers of his free hand through his hair. He glanced over at the patio where he thought I'd be, then passed his hand over his eyes. Taking up a pen, he scribbled on the pad of notepaper that rests by the phone. I could picture his small, tight vowels and consonants starkly black against the white page.

He hung up and sat for a moment, big hands on his knees, before he rose with the notepad and walked to the screen door. He's still lovely to watch in motion: walking, running, playing tennis or softball. He moved deliberately, yet gracefully, like a big Clydesdale, stepping down off the patio, striding across the grass, sitting down on the bench beside me.

"I hate this bench. No back." He stretched, and then leaned forward, elbows on the worn, dusty-blue knees of his jeans, tapping his forehead with the bound edge of the pad.

"Claire . . . that was your dad."

I tilted my chin a degree in acknowledgement.

"Your Grandma Sophia died sometime yesterday."

Aaron never was one to sugar-coat anything.

And, of course, it was really no shock. She was old, terribly old, hovering in frailty throughout her nineties. It was more of a surprise that the call hadn't come sooner.

He ran a hand up and down my back and let it rest around my waist.

"I'm sorry, babe." He rested his chin against my head for a moment. "Joe said she just died in her sleep. He talked to her the day before about groceries, went over this morning to drop them off and found her. Thought she was sleeping." I felt his lips brush my forehead, soft and fleeting as errant petals. "He's going to set the wake for Friday and the funeral Saturday."

Once again I nodded with the merest tilt of my chin.

"I'll book us some plane tickets." He stood and looked down at me for a moment. "I guess it's time you went home."

He turned and strode back toward the house, all fluid bigness, his shoulders straight and square again, his hand combing again through that white gold mane.

"We could drive." I flung the words at his retreating back.

He stopped, turned and threw me his offhand grin. "Pro-cras-ti-nation. Pro-cras-ti-nation. It's letting me wait. It's keeping me sa-a-a-a-fe," he sang to the tune of an old Carly Simon hit. He saluted me. "Nice try. We fly."

"Hotel. Not his house."

He winked. "Baby steps for my baby."

"You're a lousy singer, farm boy."

The tears didn't come as I had hoped they would, not even later, when the arrangements had been made, for bereavement fares and hotel suites and pet sitters and the holding of keys and pick-up of mail and newspapers; and after seminars had been re-arranged and graduate student consultations postponed; when all the piles of things that we call our lives had been filed into temporary holding bins and the house was dark and the bed was soft and the complacent, fat tabby was nestled in the crook of my legs and the nervous, skinny calico was tucked against Aaron's feet. When it was quiet but for the whispery stirring of infant leaves and the sweet and sad breathings of the flute next door, then I wanted to cry; I yearned for the hot, salt-water kisses, the trembling, achy, convulsive body caught in a heaved breath, and the smothering comfort of a face pressed into a pillow to keep the quiet. But I didn't. I couldn't. I hadn't in a very long while.

Another small piece of the fabric of my early life gone, ripped away. *Why cry over it?* What little was left was so frayed and faded the pattern was almost indistinguishable. It was so ugly I had tried to throw it away years ago, and told myself I didn't care, because the square of fabric upon which I now stitched was a stronger cloth that I had wove all by myself. It was Aaron and Tally who had rescued that old fabric from the scrap heap, who held out a hope the fibers might somehow be repaired. So I had locked it away in the dim attic of memory. Now, awake in the night, I clung to that fabric even as it unraveled in my fingers, even as I wondered: *Why am I doing this? I don't want to do this.*

But I could shed no more tears.

The flight from St. Louis to Chicago takes less than an hour on a good day with a tail wind. You're up, sip your soft drink, and you're down. It can take longer to get out of O'Hare and down to the Loop if the traffic on the Kennedy Expressway is especially bad. We crawled along in the rental car, marveling at the difference between rush hour in St. Louis and rush hour in Chicago, strangers returning to a strange land, expatriates come again to the homeland, twenty years later, bug-eyed at the changes. The river of cars flowed slowly toward the delta of skyscrapers, the Sears Tower, the John Hancock, the Emerald City skyline of my childhood, but there were considerably more towers looming now, nameless ones, crowding together, bumping shoulders.

"I think we're in Oz now," I murmured.

Tally cracked away at her gum, its strawberry essence filling the little sedan. "Surrender Dorothy," she drawled, leaning forward, her chin resting on my seat back.

Aaron grinned. "When we get to the Loop, it's okay to gawk and crane your neck to see the building tops. We're rubes, you know."

She was trying hard not to be impressed. "No gawking," she sniffed. "It's 1999, not 1899, and we're not country bumpkins visiting the big city."

But at the hotel she was disappointed that we weren't boarded on the lake side, sounding ever so much like Miss Lucy Honeychurch in her quest for a room with a view.

"I would have liked to see a Lake Michigan sunrise," she grumbled, her forehead pressed to the pane that offered only buildings and grids of streets stretching west into the early twilight.

"When do you ever get up to see the sunrise?" I mocked.

"I'm up every day. You know, like, for school."

"The times when I'm over, it seems like you spend more time admiring yourself in the mirror than any sunrise."

"You're not always there, are you?"

That left me with my mouth open but temporarily without words to fill the gap. Aaron glowered. It was sore spot with him, and she knew it. It used to bother her more—why her mother and father weren't married—the convoluted explanations she'd have to give to playmates and teachers: *no, they're not divorced, they just never got married; no, they don't live together, but she stays over a lot and we sometimes stay over there.* Realizing that it bothered him, too, perhaps even more so, she lately had begun to wield it as a weapon.

My aim was true on the mirror issue. She did spend a lot of time at her toilette. But then, why not? She is her father softened and molded into a feminine form, tall, a golden Palomino of a girl; Thalia, the grace of Good Cheer.

Finally Aaron choked out a retort. "Name me the last time you saw a St. Louis sunrise. Hey, you want to see a real sunrise, you come out with me to Cahokia. Now there's a sunrise."

A sigh of exaggerated weariness. "That's so like a dad."

"I am a dad."

"Are we going to see Grandpa Joe tonight?"

"Tomorrow," I said quickly. "At the wake."

"But—"

Her father headed her off at the pass. "Tomorrow," he reiterated, steering her out of our room and into hers, handing her the hotel's restaurant and night-life guide in its blue leatherette binder. "For tonight, investigate dinner. Find someplace we'll all like."

His hands on my shoulders felt like anchors, holding me in place. "Almost home."

Through the window, car lights glowed, turn signals winked red under the topaz shimmer of streetlights. Concrete heaved, asphalt flowed, glass and steel flashed neon. And underneath the colors and hard surfaces there was a low, constant thrum, the electric life of a city: cell phones, beepers, Palm Pilots, laptops. People talking and showers spraying and toilets flushing and horns beeping and whistles blowing and elevators whirring—and under that cacophony, below it all, the lapping, liquid, inexorable, hungry, yearning siren song of the water.

"My home is 300 miles away."

It drew me in the morning, called impatiently to me as I laced up my running shoes, pushed me through the revolving door of the hotel into the brisk air, pulled me along the concrete and through the early rush hour jostle of taxi cabs and pedestrians with bleary eyes and resolute mouths, into and out of the flatulence of articulated buses inching along the pavement like monstrous irradiated caterpillars. When the streets ended and the grassy sprawl of Grant Park began, I could see it just beyond, a dark, roiling green-gray mass beneath the breathier, misty gray of the clouds. Crossing Lake Shore Drive, I saw it in all its sullen glory and felt the ancient chill in the northeast winds that came tearing down the length of it from those northern locales with exotic names: Manistique, Muskegon, Munising. I should have gone north to spite the wind while I was still fresh but I turned south instead, some vestigial homing instinct setting my course. The wind pushed me along past the sailboats and cigarette boats and miniature yachts that shifted and sighed as waves swept through the harbor.

Things had changed. The Drive, which in my childhood had split in two and wound east and west around the white limestone shoulders of the Field Museum, had been moved to the west. A wide green lawn stretched where the concrete and asphalt had once lay and I marveled at man's ingenuity and nature's triumph. The Shedd Aquarium sported a curved wall of glass on the lakeside like a sheath of funky, ultracool, wraparound sunglasses. Swinging back around and heading north, I could see Navy Pier jutting out into the lake, looking alive and faintly garish, with an enormous Ferris wheel rising up and anchoring its horizontal span like a captain's wheel on a quarterdeck. Staring into the visage of the Loop, at its bared, jagged teeth of steel and glass, took my breath away as much as the force of the wind in my face.

My city was gone. And some other thing had risen in its place. Oh, it was breathtaking, the towers defiant under the leaden clouds, but also breath taking, leaving no space to breathe amid the looming surge of concrete as immovable as some neighborhood bully. The lake roiled, the buildings leaned in and then it began to rain. And the city hissed.

The funeral home squatted on a corner of the Southeast Side facing a vacant stretch of dirt and rubble slowly being reclaimed by urban vegetation: trees of heaven and thorny spurge, wide swaths of dandelions in full yellow glory. The Skyway rose beyond like the skeleton of some giant amusement park roller coaster. Conveniently, a tavern crouched on the opposite corner, belching its peculiar odors, promising relief for those who like to drown their sorrows after—or during—an evening spent across the street.

The parlor was the same—blessedly, cursedly—it hadn't changed in nearly 30 years. Oh, the carpet was different, but it was still the same worn beige, the traffic patterns of mourners clearly embedded in the industrial strength fibers, a runway down the center between rows of brown vinyl-padded folding chairs, a taxi area in front where the caskets rest, permanent indentations marking the placement of the kneelers. The sofas and armchairs were different but the same, blue and beige now, striped and solid, instead of the rose tones of before, but still faded and bearing the same, minute, tell-tale stains, brown spots of spilled coffee, yellow blooms of sweat, a purple blotch—spillage from a child's juice cup? The walls were different but the same, a dingy off-white. The crack that had fascinated me long ago had been plastered over but a new one had taken its place.

Even the casket at the far end of the room seemed familiar, the gleaming gray surface begging to be caressed, yet forbidding, too, in its highly polished silence.

And then there was my father, who should have looked familiar above all else, comfortable as an old shoe, inviting as a well-worn easy chair, but who instead was foreign territory, standing in his charcoal-gray suit that looked a little too big, the shoulders drooping a tell-tale fraction of an inch, the sleeves hanging a little too far below the wrists, the cuffed pants covering a bit too much area of shoe.

"That's not his suit," I whispered to Aaron as we paused at the entrance to the room.

He was bent over the condolence book, adding our names. He had pressed me to call my father when we got into Chicago, just to chat, but I'd resisted. So now his hand was on the small of my back, propelling me forward, guiding me as if in a dance down that center aisle past the three or four other mourners who had already arrived, viewed, condoled and staked out their territory for the rest of the late afternoon and evening. Aaron's hand gently compelled me onward, and then brought me to rest in front of the man in someone else's suit who was, indeed, my father.

He turned his head from the condolence of an elderly couple who leaned heavily on their matching canes and smiled. It was the same smile that had thrilled me as a child when he flashed it my way, bestowing it like a king's largesse. And then I was a child again—and I hated that feeling—and it seemed to go on forever, the smile and the thrill and the resentment all tangled up in the two feet of air between us.

Aaron broke the spell, extending first his right hand and then wrapping his left arm around my father's shoulder, shaking hands and pressing the flesh in a perfect man-hug.

"Joe, good to see you, though I'm sorry it's under these circumstances. You look good."

"Well, old man, you look older," came my father's reply.

They grinned like old friends, these two men who had only seen each other thrice in a span of 20 years, their communication limited to scattered phone calls at birthdays and holidays.

Then my father looked past me to Tally, hovering behind, the nervous child undermining the fledgling woman.

"There she is, and more beautiful than her pictures." He folded her in a tentative embrace but she was surprisingly willing to hug back, giving him a glancing kiss on the cheek as well, quickly wiping away the little pink smudge that her lip gloss left on his pale skin.

What is up with that?

I had sent no recent photographs. Lord knows what went on under their roof, ten blocks from my own. I made a mental note to conduct an interrogation later.

He turned his focus on me and the space between us felt impenetrable, more lead than air. But there was Aaron's hand again, the steady pressure, the irresistible force that moved its object. The hug and brush of lips against cheek were over in a matter of seconds on my part, but my father lingered in that moment, his hand replacing Aaron's on my back, pressing me against his chest until there was nothing to do but surrender my face to the soft fold of his lapel and feel the rapid thrum of his heart in my ear and through my cheek.

"Claire," was all he said.

If he wanted to say more, he didn't and I didn't let him, for at the first sign of release, the first lessening of pressure from his hand, I eased away and made my way up to the casket. The brown velveteen on the kneeler was faded and splotched, having absorbed from the tears and sweat of countless mourners. The scent of death was strong, but it wasn't the rank odor of decay, just the peculiar sweetness of institutionalized flowers: the forced freshness of gladiolus and bridled spice of carnations; that concentrated floral essence found only in the coolers of florists' shops and surrounding the dead in funeral parlors.

She was ancient, Grandma Sophie, but then she always had been, to me. She looked the same as I remembered, hair floss white, but still in the braids she always wore wrapped neatly around her head, her face a cosmetologist's nightmare of folds, lines and creases, her hands in repose all airy bones and transparent, paper-thin skin peppered with fawn-colored age spots, weighted down with the black globes of her rosary beads and the rococo silver crucifix that rested on her ridged, yellow thumbnail.

Sophia was baptized Zofia in 1903 in Poland and lived by that name until an immigration official changed it to the more conventional spelling. In the heyday of immigration, Greek, Italian, Polish, Irish, German, they were all the same. Come to the New World, change your fortune, change your name, marry, live, give birth, raise your family, grow old, die, and be surrounded by all the blooming artificiality we can muster.

"One more year, one more year and you could have bragged that you stood in two centuries, Grandma. I should have brought you crushed lilacs and lilies-of-the-valley." I bent to kiss her powdered cheek with a pinch of trepidation, for fear she would crumble into dust.

After we paid our respects, we sat on the sofa against the wall, rather than in the folding chairs. It afforded a view of the entire room and the trickle of mourners in and up to the casket. They wore faces vaguely familiar and undeniably strange. I could also watch my father as he ran through his lines and blocking in the one act called "The Mother's Wake."

If Aaron is a draft horse, my father is a Mustang, all tight, wiry energy, supple-muscled, compact of bone and movement, flaring, glaring, charming-turn-on-a-dime-mean and vice versa. Black mane graying to distinction. Pockmarked cheeks under intense brown eyes that always, even in the midst of a smile, seem on the verge of a glare. Shifty-skinned, snapping at flies and fools. A stranger would never guess he was seventy-five. Sixty-five, maybe—and only because of the furrows that fanned out from the corners of his eyes and settled around his mouth like parentheses, and the skin that drooped under his eyes, the baggage of his life and the force of gravity weighing his flesh down. But not sapping his energy. The years hadn't granted him repose: his fingers were still in his pockets, jangling his keys and change, his eyes were still scanning the perimeter of the room, making note of the available exits.

But he went through his paces like a show pony or a glad-handing politician, grippin' and grinnin', good ol' jocular Joe. *No tears, folks, 96 for Christ's sake, a good life, a full life, yes, and how are you doin', Mrs. Piskorowski, nice of you to come, is this the little Tiffany that used to visit her grandma next door, well, I'll be damned, you're getting married now?*

And so on. But I knew he hated it and would have rather been in the back of the room against the wall or in the corner, or, better still, across the street in the dark refuge of the tavern with one beer in his belly and another on the way. The oversized suit and the actor's mask couldn't hide that from me.

The dinner hour came. Tally's adolescent metabolism required a meal and her adolescent temperament craved relief from the tedium of meeting and greeting a parade of blood relations that for all intents hadn't existed the day before and would vanish again, like Brigadoon, in the span of 48 hours. She and Aaron left to find the kind of solace only fast food, familiar, fat-laden and salty, can provide.

Then it was me and the room, same but different, the faint hiss of polyester, the scent of the gladiolus, this time less sympathy, more reproach from the eyes of the women, curiosity mingled with disdain. The old men looked resigned, slack-faced, flesh delicate as parchment or the outer skin of onions, goggle-eyed behind their thick-lensed glasses. The younger ones, my age or less, cousins perhaps, looked Target fashionable, the women's hair still frozen in spiral perms a decade after they went out of fashion, the men in business casual instead of suits, clad in their nervous tics, hands running through hair, inside shirt collars, fingers drumming on knees, twisting wrists to check the time without any pretense of stealth, gauging how many more minutes until they could blow this popsicle stand. I didn't know them.

Two faces struck me. One smirked above a decent, navy-blue suit and red-striped tie, eyes shifting under a slick of neatly trimmed brown hair. The other face looked as pliable as clay, grayish flesh molded over hollows and jutting bones, unreadable, except for the startling curve of pink-tinged lower lip. When our eyes met, the lip trembled slightly, threatening some revelation, until big front teeth closed down over it, and a big-boned hand swept down over the face and kneaded it back into expressionless submission.

When I rose, it was ostensibly to visit the powder room, to splash water on my face and wrists. I paused in the foyer that connected the two parlor rooms. The other was unoccupied, as it had been 30 years before. So I stepped in.

Excerpt from *The Commons:*
***Book 1 — The Journeyman* by Michael Alan Peck**

Copyright © 2014 Michael Alan Peck

CHAPTER ONE: THE ALL-SEEING EYES

Paul Reid died in the snow at seventeen. The day of his death, he told a lie—and for the rest of his life, he wondered if that was what killed him.

"Don't worry," he said to Mike Hibbets, the only adult in New York City who'd ever cared about him. "I'm coming back."

Pop Mike ran the New Beginnings group home, where Paul lived. He didn't believe the lie. And Paul told himself that it didn't matter.

"Does your face hurt?" The old man leaned on his desk in the New Beginnings main office.

Paul twisted his pewter ring, a habit that announced when something was bothering him. His face did hurt—especially his swollen eye.

As did the ribs he hadn't been able to protect two days earlier, when he hit the ground, balled up, in a Hell's Kitchen alley while four guys stomped him until they tired of it. He'd tried to shield his face, where damage might show forever. But he fared just as poorly at that as the afternoon sun cast a beatdown shadow show on a brick wall and a girl stood nearby and cried.

Paul had little to say, and no one worked a silence like Pop Mike. His nickname had once been "Father Mike" due to a talent for sniffing out guilt that rivaled any priest's. He asked the New Beginnings kids to drop that name so potential donors wouldn't confuse his shelter with a religious operation. *There's no God to lift us up—we rise or fall together,* he taught them. So they compromised and shortened it.

"Five foster homes, three group homes, some street life in between," Pop Mike said.

"So?" Paul couldn't look him in the eye.

"So no one makes it through that without survival skills, which you have. And you've found a place here for four years, and now you're just up and leaving."

The desk was a relic of the building's days as a school, a general hospital, and before that, a mental hospital. Its round wood edge was uneven and worn, as if the many kids trapped in this chair over the years had stared it away, varnish and all.

Paul shifted in the chair, his side one big ache. He hated hearing his life recited as if it were recorded and filed somewhere, which it was.

The winter wind forced its way through the gaps between the cockeyed window sash and its frame. A storm was due.

Outside, the fading daylight illuminated the wall of the adjacent building. A cartoon-ad peacock, its paint battling to hang onto the decaying brick, peddled a variety of Pavo fruit juices.

"New Beginnings matters to you." Rumor was, Pop Mike could go weeks without blinking. "Look how you tried to save Gonzales."

"I told him to run for help. He just ran." Paul had practiced this conversation—how it would play out. Pop Mike wouldn't mind that he was leaving. If he did, Paul wouldn't sweat it.

Yet he was unable to face the man.

The painted peacock smiled despite its sentence of death-by-crumbling. Its tail, gathered in one fist, bent outward in offering. The feathers ended in a once-vibrant assortment of bottles spread above the Pavo slogan like leaves on a branch of a shade tree: "Wake up to the rainbow! Wake up to your life!"

Decades of sun and rain had rendered the flavors unidentifiable in the grime and washed-out hues. Paul could only guess at grape, apple, orange, and watermelon.

"You could apply for our Next Steps program—work your way to an equivalency credential."

Paul didn't bother to refuse that one again.

Pop Mike followed his gaze. "The all-seeing eyes."

"What?"

"The peacock. In some Asian faiths, it's a symbol of mercy and empathy. In others, it's the all-seeing eyes of the Almighty. What that one sees, of course, is a customer."

"It's time for me to go." Paul touched his fingers to his eye, which flared in protest. "This is how New York chose to tell me." He prodded the bruise to see if he could make it hurt more. He succeeded.

Pop Mike reached across the desk, took hold of Paul's wrist, and gently pulled his hand away from his face. He didn't let go until he was convinced Paul wouldn't do it again. That was the only way he could keep Paul safe from himself.

"Please," he said. "That's the one word I have left. It won't work, but I'm saying it. Please."

Paul twisted his ring.

Pop Mike took in the beaten-up backpack at Paul's feet, the military-surplus coat thrown over the back of the chair. "Where are you going?"

"Away. I'll let you know when I get there."

Wake up to your life, said the peacock.

The three-block walk to Port Authority seemed to triple in the stinging wind. Paul's military-surplus coat was suitable only for motivating the troops wearing it to prevail before winter. It came from a pallet of stuff donated to New Beginnings as a tax write-off. He'd thought the coat would keep him warm and make him look tougher. The bite of the air and the beating in the alley proved him twice wrong.

A radio, its volume cranked up to the point of distortion, hung from a nail on a newsstand, dangling over piles of papers and magazines draped with clear plastic tarps. A weather-on-the-ones update milked the conditions of the approaching storm for drama, as did several headlines. "Blizzardämmerung!" screamed the *Daily News.* "Snowmageddon!" warned the *Post.*

The stand's owner, his face framed by graphic novels and tabloids binder-clipped around the window of a dual-pane Plexiglass wall, sung about how he'd just dropped in to see what condition the conditions were in. Commuters trying to beat the weather home paid him no mind.

By now, the meteorologist was more reporter than forecaster. Rounding the corner at Forty-second and Eighth, Paul had to blink away hard-blown flakes.

A feral-looking girl pulled one of the terminal's heavy glass doors open against the wind and held it for Paul as he swept into the stream of business-people headed for the buses within. She shook a jingling paper cup at him, but neither he nor his fellow travelers dropped anything in.

Paul was relieved that he didn't know the girl, but as he angled through the rush of commuters, he chided himself for ignoring her. He'd worked those doors in more desperate times. He knew what it meant when people were kind enough to part with a few coins—and what it meant when they weren't.

Getting past the beggars meant going head-down at a steady pace. Paul was holding money, so he didn't want to see anyone who knew him. The big ones wouldn't try to take it from him in a public place, but the smaller ones could talk him out of some.

"One way to San Francisco, please," he told the woman behind the ticket-counter glass after waiting his turn. She laughed at something the man working the adjacent line said.

He couldn't hear either of them through the barrier. That was the way of Port Authority and the world beyond for the children of the streets—for the concrete kids. The people with something to smile about did it in a world built to keep you out.

She slid Paul's ticket and change through the gap under the glass. He counted the bills against his chest to see how much was left, keeping his cash out of view.

There wasn't much to hide. He was nearly broke.

CHAPTER TWO: TRINA AND THE TRAVELIN' SHOES

Annie Brucker sat on the floor of the Port Authority basement, waiting in line for gate two. Leaning against the wall, she read aloud to her five-year-old son, Zach. She held the book, *Trina and the Travelin' Shoes,* with one hand. With the other, she kept a cat's-eye marble rolling back and forth across the backs of her fingers.

She'd been doing this for forty-five minutes, flexing her knee to keep it from going stiff. Her throat burned from speaking. Her fingers ached. But she kept it up for him.

Success with the marble meant Zach watched it instead of withdrawing to his inner place. If he didn't withdraw, then he might listen. Keeping him engaged was worth the discomfort, and Annie chose to believe he was paying attention because she had no proof that he wasn't.

Their matching red hair marked them as mother and son to anyone who might have noticed them waiting in line. And whoever did notice would have been shocked to know how much sitting cost her—that a thirty-something mom suffered from advanced osteoarthritis.

That was because they wouldn't have imagined this pleasant-looking woman held down on a table by three men working hard to keep her there while she screamed, her leg filled with nails, ball bearings, and other shrapnel too tiny and blown out to identify.

"Trina took one step and was gone from her little bedroom—gone from her little house," Annie read. Zach watched the marble. "With the next step, she left the town of Jarrett, where she knew everyone and everyone knew her." The legs of the passing commuters flickered light and shadow across the pages. "The shoes didn't tell Trina where they were going, and they never asked permission to take her there."

The H.M.O. doctors in Newark said Zach suffered from autism. The V.A. doctors wouldn't go that far because they weren't equipped to deal with children, and certainly not kids like him. The experts in San Francisco would tell her more.

Annie didn't want to know about autism. She wanted to know about Zach. Did he suffer? Was he happy, or was he lost? Was he truly autistic, or was that the easy answer for doctors chasing a goal of how many patients to see in a day?

"Trina watched the trees flow beneath her, step by step," she read. "Up and over, over and up, she and the travelin' shoes went." The marble traveled along with Trina—west to Annie's little finger, east to her thumb.

The flickering of the moving legs was a distraction. So was the knee, which didn't approve of her choice of seating. When the two tag-teamed Annie, that was all it took.

The marble went rogue, clacking to the floor and rolling away. She reached for it and missed, and Trina and her travels piled on. The book slipped from her hand, her place in it lost. Cursing to herself, she fought her way to her feet.

A fast-moving commuter, lost in his texting, kicked the marble. It bonged off of a recycling bin and fled into the shadows of a vacant bus gate.

Annie limped across the terminal floor, dodging people, and ventured into the murk. Bending to grope the floor in the dim light near the empty gate, she looked back to check on Zach.

He gazed into the air to his left—already gone.

She needed that marble. No other would do. To hold her son's attention, it had to be a certain mix of blue, green, and white. It had to be a cat's-eye.

Zach knew when it was a replacement, and it took him days to adjust. Until he did, she lost him.

Annie walked her hands across the tile, through candy wrappers and empty corn-chip bags. A few feet in, she clipped the marble with her pinky. It escaped and clicked off a wall.

Further into the gloom she went, patting the varying textures of the floor. She was damned thankful for the hand sanitizer back in her purse, assuming that hadn't already been stolen.

This was New York City. She should have taken it with her.

The noises of the concourse were transformed in the blackness. Voices came not from behind her but from the dark ahead.

"I'm trying!" an old woman cried. "I'm trying!"

Annie conjured an image of a frail figure somewhere off in the terminal. Back bent, cocooned in donated blankets, the poor lost creature was having an argument from years and years before. It was a plea to no one—an attempt to convince some greater force—or maybe just a battle with herself.

Pistachio shells.

A penny, a dime—if what she felt was U.S. currency.

An empty box of some gum or candy called Gifu, its label hardly legible in the bad light.

And there, at last, was the marble, which allowed itself to be captured fair and square. She stood to return to Zach.

The victory fell away from her.

More commuters had entered the concourse. Many more. Flowing four-deep, they blocked her view entirely.

She pressed into the current of people, the tide of sharp-cornered briefcases and interfering backpacks, trying to catch a glimpse of her son. "Excuse me, please." It was just something she said—a talisman. It had no measurable effect.

"Zach?" A sidestep. "Pardon." A dodge. She caught sight of their bags.

He was gone.

"Zach?" The voice was nothing like hers. "Zach!"

One of a pair of teenage girls looked up from her smartphone and pointed down the line of ticket-holders. Zach stood alone at the bend, where the queue folded in upon itself like a millipede.

He watched a skinny kid in an army jacket who used a pack as a cushion. The boy, a teen from the looks of him, was up against the wall, eyes closed, unaware that he had an audience.

Annie calmed herself. If she allowed Zach to see her upset, he would be frightened, too. Despite all of the things he screened out, he was quick to adopt her moods and slow to lose them, even after she moved on. Freaking out would make the long ride ahead of them that much longer.

She took a breath and held it for a count of three.

###

"Zach?"

The voice ended Paul's attempt to doze through the wait for the bus. Napping was impossible in Port Authority. Faking it could stop people from bothering you, but not often enough.

A pretty red-haired woman stood behind a little kid who was staring at him.

"Whatcha doing?" she asked the boy, who Paul figured was hers. She smiled in greeting.

Paul replied with a stiff nod. Cute girls threw him off his game. Women were even worse. He knew it, and so did they.

"Who's that, Zach?" she said. "Did you make a new friend?"

"Hello, Zach," Paul said. The kid regarded him with the most serious of expressions. "What's going on, buddy?"

The woman's smile fell a little. Maybe she didn't like nicknames.

The kid turned to his mother and held his hand out, beckoning. She hesitated, unsure, but then placed something into his palm.

He offered it to Paul—a marble.

Paul liked to keep to himself on the road. Other people meant complications—delays. But this was kind of interesting. "That for me?"

No reply. The kid just kept holding out the marble.

Paul took it from his hand.

The boy looked back up at his mother, who seemed as flummoxed by her son's behavior as Paul was by her. Something important was going on, but Paul had no idea what.

The mother didn't, either. She glanced from Paul to the kid, as if there were some secret they kept from her.

He tried to hand the marble back. "He'll miss it," he told her.

The kid wouldn't accept it.

Paul gave it another try, but no. "You sure? I have to give you something, then."

The kid pointed at his ring.

"Not that." He went into his pack, pulled out his notebook and pen, and wrote "I.O.U. one gift" on a page. Tearing it out, he handed it over to the boy, who studied it.

"He doesn't do this," the mom said.

"I work with little kids at this place I live—lived. Worked. Sometimes they give me stuff."

"No. He doesn't do this. With anyone."

Paul was so terrible at reading girls—at figuring out what they meant when they said things to him. "I'm sorry," he said, because he couldn't think of anything else to say, and because maybe he'd done something wrong.

Zach held his arms out to his mother. He appeared to be satisfied with the trade.

She picked the boy up.

"I'm sorry," Paul said.

6

THE FINAL THREE AND THE BIG ANNOUNCEMENT

Anita Quinlan

INTERVIEWING THE FINALISTS

After you have narrowed down your finalists, your committee will want to get to know these authors. Once our judges had finished the first two rounds of the first Soon to be Famous (STBF) Project and winnowed the contest candidates down to the final three, we wanted to make sure that the finalists would be willing to spend the time to promote their books as well as themselves if they won. We knew that we did not want the winner to be someone who

- would not be able to relate to people on a personal level, in other words, a grump;
- could not answer questions or talk in front of an audience;
- would be inflexible with time commitments; or
- would be unable to travel to events when asked to make appearances.

Your committee will want to be proactive to make sure your winning author can fulfill certain requirements in the effort to become "famous." One of our members contacted the finalists to congratulate each of them on still being in contention while also scheduling them for a conference call with the committee. Our caller played nicely, suggesting the types of questions we might be asking. Our questions were very general, open ended enough to catch a glimpse of each candidate's personality and ability to communicate. Your committee members should ask the author finalists the following questions:

- Why did you enter the contest?
- Why did you decide to self-publish?
- Would you be comfortable discussing your book with a book club?
- Will you be available to travel?

When the time for the interview calls came, we became excited. After all, we were going to hear the live voices of our final three candidates for the first time. One member asked the questions while the rest of us listened intently and smiled a lot at each other when the candidates gave us the answers we wanted to hear. At the end of our three interviews, we breathed a collective sigh of relief and our "what if" anxiety subsided. We found that each of our author finalists

- could communicate easily,
- had a sense of humor, and
- would be able to travel and commit to speaking engagements.

PLANNING THE EVENT

Next you need to figure out the best way to announce the winner. The timing is important, and tying your announcement to a well-known library promotion such as National Library Week is a great way to catch the attention of media outlets and other library organizations. Our committee hoped linking our event to library eBook pricing, changes in the publishing industry, and the dramatic rise in self-publishing would be news—the kind of information that might capture the public's attention.

Location

Where will you hold your announcement ceremony? It could be centrally located within your contest area to make it easy for all participants to access, but it is important to make the location easy for the media to get to as well. With libraries and library groups operating on shoestring budgets these days, coming up with a location for your event will require some creativity on the financial end. This would be a great time to reach out to library organizations such as the state library association or regional library headquarters. The winning author's nominating library is another option. The important thing is to find a low- or no-cost facility that is easily accessible to the media as well as equipped with a large enough meeting room that offers any technical equipment (and hopefully assistance) you will need for the announcement.

Long before you actually ask for assistance with finding space or other financing, it will be important to build support and buy-in for your project as it unfolds. Make sure you communicate with your contacts frequently through calls, emails, and social media and in person to let them know what you are doing and why. Communicating and repeating the goals and purpose of the project to key people in your network will be essential to its overall success.

For the first STBF Illinois Author announcement, the Reaching Across Illinois Library System (RAILS) immediately stepped up to help. They hosted our announcement in their largest conference space, loaned us their video equipment (and operated it for us), and supplied other staff support. From our inception, the committee wanted the director of RAILS, Dee Brennan, to understand what we wanted to do and to accomplish. We invited her to our kickoff meeting, and she was quick to support our goals with enthusiasm. Because she was on board with our project from the start, it was much easier to go back later and ask that organization for assistance.

Adding Attention Getters

Keep using your creativity to draw attention to your announcement! Do your committee members or associated libraries have ties to a well-known author or expert associated with the library or book industry? What about an author who grew up or currently lives in your state? Would this person be willing to speak and to introduce your winning author at the announcement? Procuring a well-known speaker can add another dimension to your event and increase legitimacy for your author project. If your speaker has a following, it will again be easier to find a financial partner in the community to host an event that will dovetail with yours. Sponsors typically like to have well-attended programs. Many speakers are quite gracious about waiving their speaker fees. It never hurts to ask!

Since his message was the inspiration for the STBF Illinois Author contest, our committee wanted *Forbes* writer David Vinjamuri from New York to speak, but our committee had no money for airfare and expenses. The Illinois Library Association (ILA) supported us by agreeing to fly in our guest speaker and provide refreshments for our event. RAILS then planned a timely and strategic RAILS training workshop, open to reading advisory and content management librarians, just before our event took place. This allowed ILA to broaden the base of library personnel who could benefit from Vinjamuri's information and expertise. In other words, it created an audience for the announcement.

Extra Marketing for the Announcement

You are going to contact your usual media outlets for your announcement, such as newspapers, radio, and TV, but don't forget about libraries and library organizations. They will probably be supportive and open to helping you get the word out about your author announcement event. Most library organizations have a page on their Web sites for outside organizations and libraries to post events. Take advantage of this, as the pages are a great way to spread the word to people who will be interested in your project.

In addition to word-of-mouth marketing, use free tools like press releases to regular and key media people and special articles and eNewsletters to association members and regional and state library publications/magazine articles to spread your message. Before, during, and after the announcement, social media can be used to create drama with some well-timed pictures and teaser headlines. Remember to encourage likes and post to Twitter to create some extra buzz when the actual event is in progress. Personally invite members of the media to the event and have information ready to help them write their articles. You can plan a picture-taking session immediately after the announcement. Negotiate good prices with your local restaurant, bakery, or gift shop to provide refreshments and decorations by letting them post business signs and display business cards. With very little money and a healthy dose of librarian creativity, you can make a few homemade but memorable props to help make the event more of a celebration. Last, but not least, encourage your top three finalists to invite friends and family to help them celebrate.

RAILS opened up its marketing and promotional channels by featuring the project and the STBF announcement in its weekly RAILS eNews and other eNewsletters, targeting library staff as well as hosting the program "It's a Mad, Mad, Mad, Mad [Publishing] World: The Changing Role of the Library in the Era of Self-Publishing," which featured our special guest, David Vinjamuri.

Several of the people who attended the RAILS training did stay, as we had hoped, for the STBF presentation. We were not above bribery, enticing them to hang around by telling them there would be more comments from an interesting speaker, free food, and the results of a statewide author project.

In addition, we encouraged each of the three finalists to bring along other people. Friends and families were welcome, and we emailed library directors and/or staff from the author's submitting library asking them to attend. Committee members scrambled to invite people on Facebook groups and their personal library friends. Each of the committee members invited local press near his or her individual library to cover the event for National Library Week.

Creating Atmosphere

Make your announcement fun, intriguing, and festive—after all, it's a celebration not only of local authors, but also of your hard work! Place helium balloons in the front of the room for all to see and treat guests to a small spread of yummy refreshments.

Using a professional graphic artist to design some fun pieces to liven up the event is important. With your low or no budget in mind, ask for a volunteer from a library or library association. Use the pieces to show off your project during the announcement, as you will probably want to film the festivities. When you link the resulting video via social media, these professionally done graphic pieces will help make your project even more attractive to those watching the video.

During the STBF announcement, the three finalists were perched on stools so that the audience could see and hear them better. One committee member used her graphic arts skills to create a large six-by-two-foot banner (paper over cardboard). This banner served as a decorative prop during the event, mounted behind the authors. We took it down quickly and reused it for the photo shoot afterward. The graphic banner featured our STBF logo and large photos of five famous authors. There was just enough space on the end of the banner for one more photo. Instead of a face, however, it held a big question mark on a piece of paper covering a photo underneath. Under the question mark was our winner's photo, hidden until the winner was announced. At the moment her name was called, we pulled the cover off the question mark and let everyone see her smiling face.

We also blew up the cover photos of each of the author's books to approximately two by four feet. Each author sat directly in front of his or her book's cover while speaking. (Photos of this are available at https://www.flickr.com/photos/124428358@N05/).

We were very thankful for the support and financial backing we received from both ILA and RAILS. The event was far more memorable and festive with their timely and much-appreciated support.

ANNOUNCING THE WINNER

On the day of the big announcement, make sure you have committee members assigned to different tasks. For example, if you're bringing in a big-name speaker, ask a committee member to pick him or her up from the airport, and perhaps provide a meal. After the event your guest speaker will need to be ferried back to the airport.

Contact your finalists and ask them to prepare some remarks and answers to the following questions:

- Why did you become a writer?
- Tell us about your book.
- Why did you decide to self-publish?
- Why did you enter this contest?
- What do libraries mean to you?/How have libraries been a part of your life?

You will probably want to tell your attendees why you held the contest and give your supporting partners time to make remarks. However, keep in mind that your audience is going to want to hear from your three finalists and to congratulate the winner. Therefore, make your agenda short:

- Introductory remarks (e.g., from the director of a partner organization)
- Short remarks from two committee members
- Remarks from your big-name guest speaker
- Remarks by each of the finalists (five to seven minutes each)
- The announcement of the winner
- A few minutes for the winner to speak

- Concluding remarks by the director of your local or regional library association
- Photos
- An opportunity for guests to purchase books and get them autographed by the authors

After each of the authors has spoken, it's time for the drumroll and to announce the winner. Be sure your video camera is rolling and all the authors have admirably presented themselves.

When the winner of the 2014 STBF project, Joanne Zienty, was announced, the audience clapped and cheered, and the author cried. A few committee members did, too. (Watch the YouTube video of our announcement event at https://www.youtube.com/watch?v=O8kLJexobfQ.)

After the announcement, take plenty of pictures to send to media outlets and give the authors the opportunity to sell copies of their books to attendees.

Now that you have your winning author, you just need to make that person famous. We'll tell you how we did that in the next chapter.

7

PROMOTING THE WINNER (OR ALMOST FAMOUS)

Nicole Zimmermann

LIBRARIANS ARE THE KEY TO SUPPORTING INDIE AUTHORS (OR THE MULLET IN THE ROOM)

In 2013, self-published books accounted for 32% of the 100 top selling e-books on Amazon each week, on average.
—Alter (2014)

The mullet in the room is the old-fashioned, out-of-date attitude toward self-publishing that still exists among pockets of the reading public and librarians. The new ways of doing things are effective, legitimate, and even attractive for indie authors, but have yet to be fully embraced by librarians, the public, and traditionally published authors. Self-publishing is still often viewed as the red-headed stepchild of the publishing family. There are arguments that self-published books are poorly written or that traditionally published writers write better. Yet there are poor writers and poorly written books in all published forms. "Yes, professional validation is different than reader validation, but it still is not proof that a book is 'better,' just that one person liked it. It may just mean that the book is more marketable than others, which is no measure of a book's literary longevity. But traditional published writers like this validation—they want the gatekeepers to keep defining what's good and what's bad because they want the gate to keep having the same meaning" (Baum, 2009).

I'm not a librarian. I do not have the MLS degree nor the experience, both broad and deep, that varies throughout the library, research, and literary world. I do, however, work side-by-side with librarians. I spend time at conferences, in special projects, and in daily tasks that require our teamwork and my public relations and marketing expertise. From many, though not all, there is a clear and palpable aversion toward self-published works. The point of this project is to show the influence that libraries and librarians wield in the choices that readers are making. This can happen only if the project and the indie author are embraced.

> Prepare for all reactions. One Librarian said to me, "Self-published authors don't have a publishing deal for a reason; i.e., they aren't good enough."

Most indie ventures are embraced by the public and by professionals in the same field. *American Idol* and *The Voice* celebrate the amateur/undiscovered singer. Etsy, DaWanda, and ArtFire support the craftspeople, designers, and artisans of the world. And then consider movies. It's a bit of a feather in your cap to be part of a great indie film. When Robert Redford launched the Sundance Film Festival, the idea was to support diversity and new talent and embrace doing things in a way that mainstream Hollywood wasn't able to do. Thirty-some years later, Sundance has helped to create the idea that "indie" means thoughtful, rich, uncommon, and purposeful. It's a place the populace clamors to get into and an approach the famous clamor to buy into (and act in). (Figure 7.1 is from our second "indie" film promoting the project.)

Indie authors are everywhere. Let's face it, changing times and all . . . the Internet and publishing sites have made it easier for more authors to get their works into more readers' hands. These changes in publishing and attitudes

Figure 7.1. "Enthusiastic Librarian" Soon to be Famous video instruction shoot; Jeannie Dilger, ILA president, director at La Grange Public Library. Credit: Denise Raleigh.

have been a subject of interest for a while now. Author and New York University instructor David Vinjamuri (2012) has noted, "[T]he conceit that Indie authors are merely a bunch of lazy hacks unwilling to face rejection ignores the fact that even the biggest proponents of the old publishing system admit that there are many talented published authors nobody has ever heard of."

I bring up this timely and interesting debate between traditional and self-publishing because so much of this project relies on the support, the embrace, and the interest of librarians and other library staff. Our project was embraced by librarians across the state, who volunteered to serve as judges; some of them are pictured in figure 7.2.

Figure 7.2. Librarian judges at the 2014 Soon to be Famous announcement. Left to right: Elizabeth Hopkins, Lisle Library District; Becky Spratford, Berwyn Public Library; Marlise Schiltz, St. Charles Public Library; Tish Calhamer, Gail Borden Public Library District; Lynnanne Pearson, Skokie Public Library; Julie Stielstra, Northwestern Medicine Central DuPage Hospital. Credit: Nicole Zimmermann.

ALMOST FAMOUS

Here's where the rubber hits the road. As the title of the project states, the goal is to make your winning author famous. Well, okay, let's take an honest look at this. Famous? Maybe not, but you can certainly expect to keep him or her busy with press interviews and library appearances. If you can get your author noticed, he or she is likely to sell more books. If the author's desire is to get signed by a big publisher, then getting his or her book in more hands and getting face time with the public is more likely to make that happen. Whether at the beginning of this project or at its final stages, you will benefit from buy-in from library staff and librarians. The people on your front lines have the most impact on and connections with the public. Let's take a look at some of the avenues you can take to get your winning author's name, face, and book out there for the world to see. Getting libraries to host your winning author, and securing interviews with media, are ways to start him or her on the road to fame. (See figures 7.3 and 7.4.)

If you are considering tackling this project or have just started, hopefully you have already begun strategically planning how you will secure recognition for your author. Or if you started the project months ago and waited until now to read this chapter, you are realizing that the work has just begun. If this is the case, you are in the same boat the STBF Illinois Author committee was in when we jumped feet first into the project and were a little flummoxed by the idea that, after a winner was chosen, the real work of marketing the author had just begun!

One library director refused to support the STBF project because "It'll ruin our reputation."

I can't say it enough: the honest truth is that you need other libraries behind you to be successful. That statement actually is true for the entire project, not just for the promotion of the winning author. If your circle is well informed,

Figure 7.3. Joanne Zienty, Wheaton Public Library. Credit: Larry Pincsak.

Figure 7.4. Joanne Zienty, interview with Steve Bertrand, WGN Radio. Credit: Larry Pincsak.

they will be more likely to be on board and enthusiastic. Heralding the author to the public starts with educated library staff members! So the first step is getting the word out.

Wow, I Can Actually Use Those Business Cards I Collected at the Last Conference!

Let's take a look at connections you already have. If you are part of a library system, then that is a great place to start. Work with your state, county, university, or other system to look for sponsorship in the form of monetary support. Seek assistance through the use of their communications and publications, which likely possess a reach of more breadth and depth. For example, the STBF Illinois Author Project partnered early on with the Illinois Library Association (ILA) and Reaching Across Illinois Library System (RAILS), our library consortium for support. Both RAILS and ILA allowed us to advertise the project, the winner, upcoming appearances, and requests for program venues through their printed and digital communications.

Search your brain and your contact list for other associations and organizations to which you can sell the story of the winning author and the reasons they should want him or her to visit their libraries. Does your library system have a marketing group? Directors' club? Are there continuing education classes? Are you are part of a reference, readers' advisory, programmers, young adult, or children's networking group? Any of these can provide avenues to get the word out about the project and the winning author.

If You Can't Take Your Author on a Rainbow Tour, at Least Create a Press Kit

So you probably don't have the money or the time that Eva Perón had for her famous European Tour, but you can certainly glom onto the idea behind it. Look for ways to get facts about your newly minted STBF winner into the hands and minds of the people who will most be able to talk him or her up. To get the ball rolling for our first winner's ride to fame, the team used our connections with peers in Chicagoland libraries like the ones seen in figures 7.5 and 7.6. We presented a fact sheet—a little press kit of sorts—about our author to spur interest from our peers and press. Think about Evita's Rainbow Tour; giving people a taste of the author will leave them wanting more. Your kit could include a personal bio, "insider" fun facts about the book or writing process, a calendar of events and appearances, and contact information for the author or his or her publicity team to make sure no possible engagements are missed.

All right, a press kit may be grandiose for your budget or your plan. Traditionally, a press kit is a package of promotional material designed to inform the media about a product, person, or service. More accurately, you may not be providing information to the press, but to libraries, schools, or other target

Figure 7.5. Announcement of speaking engagement at Dundee Library. Credit: Larry Pincsak.

Figure 7.6. Joanne Zienty with her book display at Gail Borden Library. Credit: Larry Pincsak.

audiences. (For more information on press kits and how to create one, please see the resources at the end of this chapter.)

Show 'em Why it Matters (or Tie 'em to the Rails)

I'm doing this in the spirit of the Season.
—a librarian

Great, now that that is done, you need to work on getting the libraries involved. Many of them will have participated in the judging and book submittal stages, and the ones you missed will hopefully hear your "winning author" message by publication, press kit, or word of mouth through the committees you worked so hard to inform, as mentioned previously. The goal here is to get libraries to set up author talks, book signings, and other programming involving the on-site presence of your winning author. A podcast interview held at Gail Borden Library (see figure 7.7) did triple duty by getting library staff directly involved with our winner, having a social media presence, and hosting in a public area for prime exposure.

This is a strategic step. Word-of-mouth information is not only the fastest moving but also the most effective. When librarians and library staff are informed about something, they talk about it. Create an "elevator speech" for the staff so everyone feels they can explain the project. No one likes to feel ignorant or put on the spot. Help library staff and help your project by supplying them with

Figure 7.7. Big Questions podcast, Gail Borden Library. Credit: Larry Pincsak.

quick talking points. Over-the-desk-marketing is your ticket. When patrons have a chance to meet an author and get programming and reading recommendations from a library staff member, they will be more likely to attend that program and read that book. **And once again, that's the point of this project: showing the influence that libraries wield on the choices that readers are making.**

Get Ready for Your Close Up (or Media, the Necessary Evil)

The goal of social media is to turn customers
into your personal evangelist.
— Shane Barker, ShaneBarker.com

If you are reading this book, there's a good chance you are involved in marketing your library in some way. Whether you are a director, a programmer, a reference librarian, a trustee, or the communications professional at your library, you will need to consider the connections you already have, dust off those networking skills, and go to work.

Ideally, at the beginning phases of this project you should establish a few important and strategic action steps.

Web Site for Your Project—From the beginning you have diligently kept up-to-date information about coverage on the project or author. You continue to promote the winner through updates on a calendar of appearances by the author.

Social Media—When the winning author was announced during a press event in April 2014, the Soon to be Famous committee did real-time Tweets and photos of the finalists and winner. Between the committee, our guest speaker, and attendees from various libraries and ILA, we tweeted and retweeted strategically to publishers, news outlets, and library vendors and customers. Whether it's Twitter, Facebook, or Instagram, it's very important to remain in the moment with social media. Assigning a committee member to post about events and appearances in real time is imperative.

The Not-Dead-Yet Print Media and Their Online Brethren—Here's where you really have to shine up those networking skills. With fewer and fewer newspapers in print, there are fewer reporters to pester for attention. Many publications are moving to online community news, which allows you to post articles and events online without going through a reporter. However, the bang for your buck still comes with the reporter-driven story. Only these publications can determine how many eyes have the potential to view your news. You should beg, cajole, woo, and beseech to get your news "above the fold."

Show Me the Money

Even though this project doesn't have to demand a lot of funding, let's be serious—you'll go farther with more money. I think we first realized that money would come in handy when we wanted to print some materials: bookmarks, posters, flyers, winning-book award seals, oversized book covers for three finalists on announcement day—the list goes on. Think early on about whom you can approach for sponsorship. This can mean either in-kind donations (e.g., free or at-cost printing, free meeting space) or cold cash. Is there an association you can call upon, a local bookstore, a printer your library does a lot of business with, or a business that supports literacy? Perhaps you even know an author who was once self-published and made it big. Don't be shy about asking. All anyone can do is say "no," and you'll be surprised how many will say "yes."

WORDS FROM OUR WINNER JOANNE ZIENTY (OR EVERYBODY'S GOT A PITCH FOR A SCRIPT)

Hollywood always likes a good sequel (or three or four). (You know, built-in audience . . . creative bankruptcy . . . the constant search for a few more dollars. . . .) And so let's be a fly on the wall in the glistening corner office of a studio in LA and listen in on the pitch meeting for *Soon to be Famous, Part II: Adventures in Library Land*.

Screenwriter:

So the first was a big success. You know, Demi won the Oscar for best actress. So, I'm thinking . . . sequel. Here's the thing—we follow her on her struggle for acceptance in the brutal world of collection development . . . her journey through the dark underbelly of public libraries.

Big Shot Hollywood Producer:

You think? I mean, when I think of libraries, I don't necessarily think "dark underbelly."

Screenwriter:

Oh, you'd be surprised. I mean, our heroine is going to have to deal with the fact that there's still a stigma with self-published authors—even in the twenty-first century, the day of YouTube, Vine, etc., etc. Anyway, here's the plot. Our heroine wakes up to find she's a semi-hot commodity in the media world. We'll do a montage of her interviewing with a couple of local and national radio stations. I'm picturing her in downtown Chicago, crossing the river, whatever the name of the river is, and looking up at the Wrigley Building. Maybe we'll have her do the Mary Richards thing and toss her hat.

Big Shot Hollywood Producer:

Mary Richards?

Screenwriter:

You know, the *Mary Tyler Moore Show*? (*Blank look from producer*) Well, anyway . . . she's interviewed on these radio shows and gives a number of interviews to local newspapers, too. One of them is even a podcast that's recorded at a library. We can get the Gail Borden Library in someplace called Elgin, Illinois. It's a very hip place. We can do some cool set and art direction. I'm thinking we'll set it up with a great display case that's based on all the artifacts mentioned in the book. We'll shoot a scene with our heroine "oohing" and "aaahing" over that display case. It'll be great, great. And maybe we can get Brad Pitt—no, Chris Hemsworth—to play the interviewer. We'll call the show "The Big Questions." It'll be an awesome scene, lots of atmospherics. We'll show our heroine with a case of nerves beforehand, sitting out in her car to pump herself up beforehand. Drama, lots of drama. Then, we can show her listening to herself on YouTube afterward. Laughs, lots of laughs.

Big Shot Hollywood Producer:

Okay, and then what?

Screenwriter:

Um, well, we'll have a few scenes showing her blogging on her experiences and accepting email invitations to appear at libraries. We'll do an old-school calendar page flip, except instead of a print calendar, it'll be a Google calendar.

Big Shot Hollywood Producer:

(Nods) Okay, okay. And then?

Screenwriter:

(Feeling a little pressured) And then a few scenes showing the sales of her book climbing on Amazon and Smashwords . . . and a few scenes showing her dragging her little suitcase full of books around and sometimes getting lost on the way to libraries and wishing she'd brought Jill, her GPS along with—comic relief, you know—and a few scenes of her actually presenting at all these different libraries. And here's the thing: in general, audiences really enjoy her presentation, but then . . . at one library . . . on a crisp night in the middle of autumn with a creepy full moon . . . . *(blissful, picturing the cinematography possibilities)* she meets up with this one guy who's sort of a . . . semi-heckler. Maybe he's bitter about the contest rules . . . because he's fixated on them not taking nonfiction entries. She explains that nonfiction needs to be vetted because . . . well, hey, it purports to be . . . you know, the truth. But he's not having it . . . and. . . .

Big Shot Hollywood Producer:

And . . . she starts to fear for her life? Is this guy a psycho stalker? *(His face is flushed with excitement.)* Or maybe he's a psycho retired publishing industry executive who views himself as the gatekeeper of the publishing galaxy and has taken it upon himself to wipe every self-published author off the face of the earth!

Screenwriter:

(Dumbfounded, staring in disbelief) Uh, no. This isn't one of those kinds of movies . . . uh . . . *(nervously)* unless we need it to be one of those kinds of movies to greenlight it. Uh, does it need to be one of those kinds of movies?

Big Shot Hollywood Producer:

No, no. I was just thinkin' out loud. You know, if it was one of those kinds of movies, we could maybe get Liam Neeson to do his "particular kind of skills" riff. *(Dreamy-eyed; you know he's seeing dollar signs.)*

Screenwriter:

Well, uh, maybe we can get Liam to be a hunky librarian instead. Or a hunky audience member who also happens to be a self-published author. Or a hunky librarian who also happens to be a self-published author AND an ex-CIA agent who still takes the occasional undercover assignment. . . .

Big Shot Hollywood Producer:

(roused from his Liam Neeson dreams) So essentially, what you're telling me is, this is a story where our heroine talks to a bunch of reporters and goes to visit a lot of libraries . . . where's the drama in that? What's the story arc?

Screenwriter:

(crestfallen) Uh, well, she's . . . she's really kinda shy. So she has to rise above that to present before these audiences. Um, and . . . and then, we show our heroine's realization and astonishment at the fact that a lot of the larger, "big name" libraries haven't invited her to present . . . and how she comes to understand that the stigma of self-publishing is still out there . . . and that how ironic is that? But then . . . and here's the big climax . . . at one of the presentations, she actually meets a reader who is moved to tears—yes, to tears— as she describes the memories that our heroine's novel provoked in her, memories of her parents' home, and our heroine is so very moved by this experience that she finds herself near tears, too . . . and the knowledge that her words had such an impact on another person . . . this is something that she will always treasure and keep in her heart, as she moves forward in writing her next book.

Big Shot Hollywood Producer:

So that's the money shot, eh? The reader and the writer connecting over this book?

Screenwriter:

Yeah, that's the money shot. And it'll win Demi another Oscar.

REFERENCES

Alter, Alexandra. (2014, January 7). Fast-paced best seller: Author Russell Blake thrives on volumes. *The Wall Street Journal.* Retrieved from http://www.wsj.com/articles/SB1000 14240527023036406045792986040444404682

Baum, Henry. (2009, May 9).Why do people hate self-publishing so much? *Self-Publishing Review.* Retrieved from http://www.selfpublishingreview.com/2009/05/why-do-people-hate-self-publishing-so-much/

Vinjamuri, David. (2012, August 15). Publishing is broken, we're drowning in indie books—and that's a good thing (blog). *Forbes.* Retrieved from http://www.forbes.com/sites/davidvinjamuri/2012/08/15/publishing-is-broken-were-drowning-in-indie-books-and-thats-a-good-thing/2/

RESOURCES

http://www.thecreativepenn.com/2013/04/23/press-kit/
http://www.westbowpress.com/AuthorHub/Articles/PressKit.aspx

8

GOING FORWARD

Lucy Tarabour

PROJECT OUTCOMES

Outcomes and assessment have become key in our professional world, and so it is with an author awards program. Documenting your success will help you gain more support in the future, and noting your failures helps you learn from them and do things differently next time around.

Level of Participation

Once you have held your awards ceremony, you'll want to evaluate the success of your program. One way to do this is by counting participants. In our case, we were thrilled to have 76 Illinois libraries sponsor 103 entries to the Soon to be Famous (STBF) Illinois Author Project, far exceeding our original goal of 25 submissions.

Did you just scratch the surface of self-published novels out there? How effective were you at getting the word out? These points are difficult to assess, but it's a good idea to keep documentation and notes, in any case—a scrapbook with any press coverage, numbers of attendees at the award, and so forth. One of our goals was and is for all the libraries in Illinois to consider themselves partners with us in promoting STBF in their communities. While many librarians embraced the project, some were either wary or just not able to spend time on it.

As you begin your second year in a project, you'll likely find there is more familiarity and consequently a higher comfort level with the whole process. As STBF becomes an annual event, we're hopeful that the increased familiarity will lead to more participation. Replication of the project in other locales will also help boost participation.

In addition, we have taken steps to make it easier for authors and librarians to submit entries while maintaining the face-to-face encounter between author and librarian. This personal contact, we believe, is a key factor in strengthening the relationships between authors and libraries and reinforcing the role of libraries as curators.

Did You Make Your Author "Famous"?

Fame is a hard thing to measure, but with 26 different library appearances, invitations to five private book clubs, interviews on WGN and WDCB radio, and participation in three conference/literary fest events on her schedule, Joanne Zienty has certainly received a lot of attention. Print articles in major newspapers such as the *Chicago Tribune* and *Daily Herald* as well as in numerous local newspapers and the *ILA Reporter, School Library Journal, Booklist Online, Forbes*, various library/publishing-related blogs, and the STBF Web site also contributed to the spotlight focused on Joanne, her novel, and the whole issue of the relationship between self-publishers and librarians.

Of course, much of the media attention we received was the result of the fact that our program was something of a novelty. As more libraries begin to launch author awards programs, it will become more of a challenge to gain certain kinds of exposure. But the hope is that new developments and twists on the idea will warrant further attention. For example, perhaps some participating libraries will come together to host a runoff among regional award winners. Or maybe someone will launch a print-only contest, or a nationwide contest for a specific genre of writing, such as mystery or memoirs. Publicity and marketing professionals can always find a great new angle or way to pitch a story.

WHAT ABOUT BOOK SALES?

Library Acquisitions

How many libraries will buy your winning author's book? Check Worldcat and note how many libraries own copies (and where they are).

In Joanne's remarks the day she won the award, she talked about this experience: "Wallowing in self-absorption, I googled my book. To my astonishment, I discovered my novel had been added to the collection of the public library in Bangor, Maine. I don't know a single soul in Bangor, Maine. But somehow, some way, some librarian deemed by book shelf-worthy." That Bangor librarian is not alone. Joanne Zienty's winning entry is now part of the collections of 110 libraries: 95 in Illinois, and 15 libraries in nine other states from Maine to California.

General Sales

General book sales are another indicator of success. Work with your winning author (and the runners up) to gather sales data. *The Things We Save* was available on Amazon and through other channels for two years before Joanne won the contest. In the first nine months after Joanne became the first STBF Illinois author, she sold seven times more print versions of the book than she had sold during the previous two years—a 600 percent increase! eBook sales through Amazon Kindle jumped almost 375 percent over the previous two years. Finally,

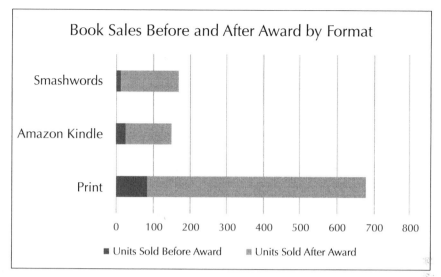

Figure 8.1. How the STBF award increased book sales

through Smashwords eBook channels, she has sold 15 times as many eBooks as she did before the recognition of Soon to Be Famous. (See figure 8.1.)

Joanne commented in an email: "I am approaching the 1,000-sold mark, which is about 999 more than I ever thought I would sell. However, I won't be satisfied until I've sold more than Snooki. Good news is, I only have about 8,000 more to go." Look out, Snooki!

WHAT WAS ACHIEVED

By capitalizing on the power and credibility of libraries, you can accomplish three things through your author awards program:

- Increase the visibility of self-published works by offering encouragement and recognition to self-publishing authors.
- Help change the public's perception of self-published books.
- Demonstrate the library's role as an authority and "gatekeeper" to identify, offer, and promote quality reading from all sources.

The third point is a particularly important one. Many libraries are getting involved in promoting self-publishing. Nate Hoffelder, editor of the blog *The Digital Reader*, writes:

Far from being a warehouse for books, a growing number of libraries are taking an active role in promoting self-publishing. This includes the Seattle Public Library, which recently launched a writing contest in partnership with Smashwords. Hartford County Public Library, which is located in Maryland, offers workshops and even hosts a writing conference. Others, like Loudoun County Public Library, have installed an Espresso Book Machine and invite local writers to have their works printed. (2014)

What is less common, however, is libraries providing a truly curated selection of self-published works. Identification of the highest quality self-published novels is a cornerstone of the STBF project and will hopefully be a part of your program as well.

STBF Projects in Other States

As the 2015 STBF Author Project in Illinois is well under way, other states are joining the movement. Our committee received inquiries from librarians in Ohio and the District of Columbia. After attending our ALA Midwinter presentation on the project, a librarian from South Carolina approached us, eager to find out more. He is now organizing a similar initiative in his home state.

PLEASANT SURPRISES

Along the way with your program, you are likely to have some pleasant surprises, as we have. Here are a couple of byproducts of STBF that we were happy to see.

Libraries Using STBF Resources in Different Ways

In truly creative fashion, library marketers are coming up with ways to make the most of the resources developed by the STBF project other than running a contest. For example, recognizing the value of the judging criteria and methods we developed, some librarians have asked us for permission to use our rubric-based scoring system in their own libraries to aid in developing their own curated collections of self-published works.

New Type of Partnership with Publishers

We were expecting (and hoping!) that other library marketers would pick up this ball and run with it, but we were heartened to find that our efforts also made publishers start to look at libraries a little differently.

Due in large part to the success of STBF during the summer of 2015, a test of publisher-supported merchandising will be conducted at a number of different libraries nationwide.

Designed to demonstrate the power of libraries to build author awareness, the focus of the project will be on midlist titles and will include curated offerings from Big Five, small press, and indie authors. Stay tuned!

Why Replication?

Let's face it. Although there are myriad creative programs, services, and tools at libraries today (and we're all for that!), our core mission and brand is all about books and reading. No librarian would dream of ignoring 40 percent of all the books published in a given year when making purchasing decisions. And yet, without some systematic way of evaluating self-published books, we're in danger of doing just that.

The advent of the eBook quickly led to an explosion in self-publishing, and sales numbers bear out the fact that these indie books are in demand. Libraries must adapt their methods of identifying the best books from ALL sources for their patrons to fulfill their mission. We offer our experiences from the STBF Illinois Author Project as a guide and a place to begin.

HOW SNOOKI FROM THE JERSEY SHORE "INSPIRED" OUR WINNER

Joanne Zienty describes how she decided to self-publish:

Most writers aren't in it for the money. We write because we are compelled to—because we have to get these characters out of our heads and onto a page, whether they spring full blown like Athena from the forehead of Zeus or whether they are dragged forth, with much pain and sweat, like the typical birth process. The day I decided to self-publish was the day I learned that Snooki, from the reality TV show *The Jersey Shore*, had a publishing deal, and presumably a ghostwriter. That killed any remaining illusions I had about the publishing industry. Paraphrasing Stuart Smalley, I thought, "It's good enough, it's smart enough and doggone it, people like it. And like Bluto says in *Animal House*: 'don't cost nothin'.'"

IN CONCLUSION

Google "But that's the way we've always done it," and you'll find pages of cautionary tales about the consequences of failure to respond to change with innovation. Remember when going to Blockbuster was a routine part of everyone's weekend entertainment? And how long has it been since Kodak was "the" brand in popular photography? Failure to adapt in a timely way to technological change was disastrous for these once-powerhouse companies.

For libraries, continued reliance on the well-established process of collection development that relies almost exclusively on the offerings of the Big Five publishers no longer works in today's literary world of eBooks and a booming self-publishing industry. We offer our experiences developing and executing the first Soon to be Famous Illinois Author Project as a model, a way to "disruptively innovate" in the face of change.

So jump in! It's certainly challenging, and perhaps a little crazy, but the rewards are great.

REFERENCE

Hoffelder, N. (2014, September 2). Kentucky public libraries launch new web portal for self-published authors. *The Digital Reader* (blog). Retrieved from the-digital-reader .com/2014/09/02/kentucky-public-libraries-launch-new-web-portal-self-published -authors/

AFTERWORD

Lucy Tarabour

We are pleased to announce that in the months since the completion of our book, the Soon to be Famous Illinois Author Project has chosen Michael Alan Peck as the 2015 winner for his novel *The Commons, Book 1: The Journeyman*.

Eighteen librarians from across the state served as volunteer judges, selecting this book from 43 self-published adult fiction entries. Michael accepted his award at a ceremony at Illinois Library Association (ILA) headquarters in Chicago on April 16, 2015, and is already scheduled to make numerous appearances at libraries, conferences, and other media events to promote his book.

Also, the members of the STBF committee were thrilled to be named recipients of the prestigious John Cotton Dana Award for excellence and innovation in library public relations for the development and execution of the Soon to be Famous Illinois Author Project.

Recognizing the power of libraries to create author "buzz," the Library Discovery Project is scheduled to roll out in 27 libraries in Illinois in the fall of 2015. Publishers and libraries will work together to raise awareness of midlist authors and their work by building on libraries' increasingly important role in the book discovery process through special marketing efforts.

Finally, a seed planted on a Chicago-cold day at the 2015 ALA Midwinter Meeting is beginning to flower in South Carolina. A brief conversation following our presentation at that event has led to a new version of STBF. To best serve the needs of their patrons and achieve the goals set to meet those needs, library marketers from South Carolina are folding the author contest into a larger project funded by a Library Services and Technology Act (LSTA) grant that also includes educational programming and follow-up initiatives that align with state goals. Again, these creative professionals are demonstrating the power of libraries to promote reading, authors, and education. How might an STBF project help you achieve your goals?

Upon receiving the 2015 Soon to be Famous Illinois Author Project award, Michael Alan Peck reflected, "Of any contest I've entered, the Soon to be Famous Illinois Author Project means the most to me. Libraries are where stories live, and librarians are the dedicated experts who guide us to our next magical read. This is the same feeling I have when absorbed in a great novel: I can't wait to find out what happens next."

Like Michael, we can't wait to see what's next!

Appendix A

PROJECT TIMELINE AND DOCUMENTATION

Julianne Stam

AS SOON AS POSSIBLE

- Assemble a committee.
  We librarians are good at networking. Our RAILS (Reaching Across Illinois Library System) Marketing Group network was the starting place for finding members to form a committee. Use your networks, both formal and informal. You'll multiply your creativity, energy, and fun!
- Bring your governing organizations on board.
  Support from Reaching Across Libraries System (RAILS) and the Illinois Library Association (ILA) was invaluable to us. It provided us with exposure, credibility, and resources.
- Set a realistic timeline.
  Use this book as a resource to plan all you need to do, including creating a Web site and social media sites, creating submission and judging guidelines, recruiting authors and judges to participate, figuring out the timing of each round of judging, and planning your announcement event.
- Set up and promote a Web site as a resource for both authors and librarians. (See soontobefamous.info for ideas.)

THREE TO SIX MONTHS BEFORE YOUR SUBMISSION DEADLINE

- Get the word out to libraries.
  Engage librarians throughout your state or library system by providing them with the tools they need to become partners in your contest. This includes press kits and graphics they can personalize and use in their communities, as well as clear guidance on their roles as "sponsors" of local authors.
- Get the word out to authors.

Send information on your contest to local author groups and any groups devoted to self-publishing. Many libraries have their own writers' groups, whose members may have a self-published book to enter in your contest. Contact local press.

- Recruit professional librarian judges.
  Use any and all professional resources at your disposal to get the word out to librarians, including local governing organizations and their communication tools.
- Establish criteria for judging entries.
  We have included judging criteria and a rubric that you can customize or use as inspiration to create your own. See Chapter 5 for more information.

DURING THE JUDGING PROCESS

- Plan your announcement event.
  Once the contest is under way, you should be planning the event at which you will announce the winner, including inviting the press to attend. Once you have reached the final round in the judging, let your finalists know the date and location of the event.
- Brainstorm promotion ideas for making your winner "famous."
  While your professional librarian judges and your committee's judging coordinator are busy with the evaluation of your entries, the rest of your committee should be working on the goal of making the winner "famous." In addition to appearances and signings at libraries, sift through all your media contacts to generate coverage in print, broadcast, and online. See Chapter 7 for more information.

AFTER THE ANNOUNCEMENT OF THE WINNER

- Contact all libraries in your system to schedule appearances for your winner.
- Evaluate and share your experiences. Look into presenting your project at library conferences.
- Begin planning the following year's event.

THROUGHOUT THE WHOLE PROCESS

- Keep your Web site up to date.
- Post regularly on Facebook.
- Constantly promote your project everywhere you go.
- HAVE FUN!

Judge Recruitment Form

JUDGING PROCEDURES
At the outset, thank-you so much for agreeing to assist with the Soon to be Famous Illinois Author Project. As we want to ensure that everyone has the best experience possible, we want to set up some procedures.

CONFLICT OF INTEREST
It is the policy of the Soon to be Famous Illinois Author Project (STBF) to avoid conflicts of interest and the appearance of conflicts of interest resulting from its activities. In particular, no person should obtain or appear to obtain special advantages for himself, his relatives, her employer, or her close associates as a result of services on a committee. A conflict of interest occurs when an individual's personal or private interests may lead an independent observer reasonably to question whether the individual's professional actions or decisions are influenced by considerations of significant personal or private interest, financial or otherwise.

CONFIDENTIALITY
STBF judging committee members need to maintain a high degree of confidentiality regarding the committee's discussions, both oral and written. All committee members need to feel free to speak frankly in a closed session, knowing that their comments will not be repeated outside that room, and that they reserve the right to speak for themselves outside of that closed session. It is important to remember that in these discussions, committee members may express only their own opinions and may not quote the opinions of other committee members or indicate in any way which books are under consideration. It is understood that all eligible books are being considered up until the selection of the winner is made. Members of the committee should not reveal or publicize any confidential information learned through service on the committee, nor should they make such confidential information available to noncommittee members.

Members of the judging committee who run or participate in social networking Web sites or software, including blogs, wikis, electronic discussion lists, and the like, should not engage in any discussions about the STBF project or about the status of eligible books during their term of committee service.

CHANGES
From time to time, the STBF committee may take other action or establish such other guidelines as may be necessary in the STBF's sole discretion to protect the integrity of the process.

QUESTIONS/COMMENTS

Any questions from authors or prospective committee members and candidates should be directed to [insert the contact information for the person on your committee who is handling this].

Ready to sign up as a judge?

I would like to participate as a judge.

Librarian Name (required): _____

Title/Position (required): _____

Your Email (required): _____

Library Name and Address (required). Please include street address, city, and zip code:

_____

_____

Your Phone Number: _____

I understand and agree to adhere to the guidelines for service on the award committee as outlined herein and agree to adhere to such other guidelines as the STBF may hand down from time to time.

    YES / NO

By typing my full name below, I agree that all information entered was done accurately and truthfully.

_____

Book Nomination Form

Welcome! We're so glad you are interested in being part of the XYZ Author Contest!

To be nominated, the book must be:

- Adult fiction [or whatever level or genre you choose]
- Self-published
- Written by an ABC resident
- Available in either an .EPUB or .MOBI file or as a free download from Smashwords, Amazon, or Barnes & Noble
- Sponsored by an ABC library (public, academic, school, or special)

Please note: An author may submit only one book. That book must be new to the XYZ project and may be nominated by only one library.

TIPS FOR COMPLETING THE APPLICATION

- Please read the entire online application first. If you start the application and cannot complete it, you will not be able to save it.
- Ask a library in ABC to sponsor your book. The librarian does not have to read/recommend/critique the book; however, he or she may. The librarian nomination form includes both of these options. Bring a copy of your book on a flash drive or CD or a hard copy to the library.
- Fill out the entire application. The application can be completed by either the author or the sponsoring library.
- Please look through the application form below and also read "I'm an Author, What do I need to do?" on our Web site. With that under your belt, you should be ready to apply.
- Good Luck! We look forward to reading your book!

Author Name LAST (required): _____

Author Name FIRST (required): _____

Author Email (required): _____

Author Address (required):

_____

_____

Author Phone Number (required): _____

Book Title: _____

Is your book adult fiction?   YES / NO

Is your book self-published?   YES / NO

Do you live in ABC?   YES / NO

Information about the book:

Information about the author:

Sponsoring Library Address and Contact Information

Sponsoring Library (required): _____

Sponsoring Library Address (required):

_____

_____

Sponsoring Library Staff Name (required): _____

Staff Email (required): _____

Staff Phone Number (required): _____

Sponsoring Library Director Name (required): _____

Sponsoring Library Director Phone (required): _____

Sponsoring Library Director Email (required): _____

My Library/Librarian will be submitting:

   Option 1: Librarian will read/skim book and give comments.
   Option 2: Librarian will sponsor entry without reading book.

Please submit your book electronically. Unfortunately, we cannot accept .PDF or .DOC files.

If you need help making your manuscript into an .EPUB file, please visit "How to make an epub file" under our FAQ heading on the right side of the Web page.

In what format will you be submitting your book?

.MOBI (Kindle) file
.EPUB file
Both formats

Book is available as a free download at Amazon/Smashwords/Barnes & Noble/Other _____

Please include a URL if we can download your book for free from Smashwords, Amazon, Barnes & Noble, etc. Downloads must be available [include date range].

Instructions to Judges on Downloading eBooks

The eBooks that you will be receiving will most likely be available in one of three ways: as an .EPUB or a .MOBI file attached to an email from the committee, as a link to a free Kindle eBook on Amazon's Web site, or as a link to Smashwords where you can choose to download the book as an .EPUB or a Kindle .MOBI file.

.EPUB is the most common eBook file format. It can be read on most eReaders and tablets (except Kindles and Kindle Fires) and on any computer equipped with Adobe Reader. The file should open easily by clicking on it in the email.

A .MOBI file is a Kindle file. If you have a Kindle, you can forward the email to your Kindle's email address. To find out the address, sign into Amazon and go to Manage My Account then Manage My Kindle Devices. While there you will also need to add the email address you are sending the email from to the list of approved senders. This should also work for Kindle apps. If you are using the Kindle app on a device such as an iPad, you should be able to open the email on the device, and then you should get the option to open the attachment in your Kindle app.

First Round Judging Guidelines

Thank you for participating as a judge for the XYZ Author Project. Attached are some reviewing guidelines and things to consider as you read the books that you have been given. Please do not feel you have to answer each of these questions in your summary; these are simply some things to think about while skimming the book. What we are looking for during this first round is a brief evaluation (only seen by the committee; **there should be no communication between yourself as a judge and the authors**) and a recommendation on whether each of the books you have been given should move along in the judging process to the next round based on your evaluation. An evaluation form is attached; please make additional copies as needed for each book.

For each book that you feel qualifies to continue, we need a brief summary of the book including your opinion of it. Each form should include the title, author, and genre. The first paragraph should include information about the characters and story. In the second paragraph please indicate who would be the general audience for this book, what you find appealing about it, and your general overall impression.

For each book that you feel qualifies as a book that **should not** move on to the second round, please list the title and author and check the box indicating that this book should not move beyond this first round.

Though some of you may not be able to give a "yes" vote to any of the books you were given, if you choose to recommend that more than one book move along in the process, please indicate which is your first choice among them and why. If you choose to recommend all that you were given, please rank them first, second, third, etc.

We plan to announce the winner on [date], which gives us a pretty tight timeline. We would like your evaluations of these books back to [your committee's judge coordinator] by [date]. This gives you about a week to skim each book and make a decision about whether it is worth having others read.

Thank you again.

The XYZ Author Committee

Soon to be Famous First Round Judging Form

Name of Judge: _____

Title of Book 1: _____

___ move to the next round of judging (review is attached)

___ This book should not move to the next round of judging.

Title of Book 2: _____

___ move to the next round of judging (review is attached)

___ This book should not move to the next round of judging.

Title of Book 3: _____

___ move to the next round of judging (review is attached)

___ This book should not move to the next round of judging.

Title of Book 4: _____

___ move to the next round of judging (review is attached)

___ This book should not move to the next round of judging.

If you choose more than one book to move to the next round, please rank them:

_____ Book 1

_____ Book 2

_____ Book 3

_____ Book 4

Reviewing Guidelines/Points to Ponder

Title:

What does it suggest?
Does the title fit the book?
Is it interesting? Uninteresting?

Book Arrangement:

Does the author provide any revealing information about the story in a preface/introduction?
How is the book arranged?
Do the chapter/section breaks make sense?
Did each chapter leave you wanting to find out what would happen next?

Genre:

What type of book is this?
Who is the intended audience for this work?
Does the book meet the expectations for its intended genre?

Characters:

Are there characters in the work?
Who are the principal characters?
How do they affect the story?
From what point of view is the story written?
Were the characters credible and fully realized?
What problems/issues did the main characters encounter? What adventures did they have?
Could you relate to or empathize with any of the characters in the story?
Who was your favorite character, and why?

Storyline/Plot:

What was the story about?
What is the setting for the story?
Is the plot of the story believable?
Was the book a "page-turner" that made you want to keep reading it?
Were there unexpected twists to the story that you enjoyed?
Is the conclusion of the story satisfying?

Themes/Motifs/Style:

> What themes or motifs stand out?
> How do they contribute to the work?
> Are they effective or not?
> How would you describe this author's particular style and use of language?
> Is the book accessible to all readers or just some?
> Is there any social commentary involved in this work?

Overall:

> Was the book proofread and spell-checked?
> Did the author follow grammatical rules and write in complete sentences?
> Did you like the book?
> What was your favorite part of the book?
> Did you have a least favorite part of the book?
> Are there things that you feel need to be changed?
> Would you recommend this book to someone?
> What type of person would like this book?
> **Will this book stand up to outside critical review?**
> **Would you recommend this book to go to the next round of judging?**
> **Would this book have mass appeal to a wide audience?**

Soon to be Famous Illinois Author Rubric

How to use this rubric:
For each row, give the book a ranking from 1–12 and enter the score in the farthest right column. Total all of the individual scortes. Fill in additional comments that will help with the evaluation process. Thanks!

Title					
Author					
	1 2 3	**4 5 6**	**7 8 9**	**10 11 12**	**Score**
Commercial Value	Bland with little commercial appeal	Interesting concept, but a bit of a yawner.	A pleasant read, but not a lot of thought provoking substance.	Highly enjoyable read that stimulates the intellect.	
Characterizations	Forgettable and dull.	Conventional, established characters.	Interesting, multilayered characters.	Fascinating, extremely well developed characters.	
Story telling	A challenge to get through to the end. Boring, confusing.	A decent story that flows fairly well.	Story stayed with me between readings.	A page turner. Was disappointed when I finished.	
Plot	Weak introduction, tepid or disorganized development. Uninspired resolution.	Mildly interesting introduction, basic/ predictable resolution.	Good introduction to set the stage; some development involving conflict, opposition, or a problem; and a decent climax and resolution	Interesting introduction to set the stage; strong development involving conflict, opposition, or a problem; and a riveting climax and resolution	
Accuracy and organization	Verbose writing, confusing to reader	Ideas not expressed clearly	Consistent writing	Concise and smooth writing, creative use of language	
Would you recommend to a patron?	I would not recommend	I might put on bottom of my reading list	I would add to my recommendation reading list	I would pre order a copy for them	
Total					
Additional Comments:					

Figure A.1 Rubric for Second- and Third-Round Judging

Appendix B

WRITING A BOOK REVIEW

Julianne Stam

Your committee will need to decide how detailed the book-reviewing guidelines for the judges will be. The reviewing guidelines given to our judges for the first round gave them points to ponder and use in the writing of their reviews. When we asked the judges to write a short review for the books moving from round one to round two, we gave them instructions to write a two-paragraph review and identify the title, author, and genre of the book. In the first paragraph, we wanted a summary of the book, including information on characters and the story/plot. The second paragraph was to identify the audience for the book, what the judge found appealing about the book, and the judge's overall impressions. For the reviews in the final round, we requested that the judges write only a few comments about the book.

Once your winner has been chosen, one of the ways in which you want to help that author become "famous" is by promoting his or her book. One of the ways to garner more attention for the book is to help the author get more online reviews. You should encourage your judges and committee members to write online reviews for your winner's (and possibly your other finalists') books. Some of the places that they can do this are GoodReads, Amazon, Barnes & Noble, Smashwords, their personal blogs, and their local library newsletters. Not every librarian or library staff member is necessarily familiar with what to include in an online book review, so you may want to share the following guidelines with them:

- Avoid spoilers. Do not give away any major plot points in your review.
- Include information on the genre of the book. Is it a romance? A mystery? Historical fiction? This is important information for many readers.
- Feel free to make comparisons to similar books: "Fans of [author name] will enjoy this book" or "If you liked [book title], then you are going to love it."
- Describe the plot and pacing of the story. Is it predictable? How quickly does it move? Is it a page turner with lots of twists and turns?
- Describe the setting. Where and when does the book take place? Do the setting and atmosphere add to the story?

- Talk about the characters. Are they well formed and realistic? Did you care about them? Did you like them? Did you have a favorite character?
- Did you enjoy the book overall, and what did you enjoy about it?
- Who would enjoy this book? Identify the types of readers who would be attracted to this book.
- Let readers know if you would read that author again and/or read more books in the series.

There is one more consideration to think about. What if the book just doesn't appeal to you or the person you are asking to write the review? As long as your review is fair and balanced, there is no reason it should not be uploaded. Increasing the number of reviews online is a good goal, and not every book is going to appeal to every person. Even slightly negative reviews can lead to sales depending on what is said in the review. If your reviews include the fact that you did not like the book because it includes time travel, someone who enjoys time travel books may try it anyway. If you have a judge who you know absolutely hated your winning entry and gave it the lowest possible score, then you may want to consider not asking that person to write a review for your winner.

Appendix C

LIBRARY MARKETING GUIDELINES AND RESOURCES

Denise Raleigh

CREATING AN OPTIMAL MARKETING COMMUNITY

If you have reached this point in the book, you realize that what we hope to achieve is to build a Soon to be Famous community. As other states and communities join the project, libraries will strengthen their relevance, helping to lead the way for customers to find good reads as the publishing landscape continues to shift. This appendix contains some general library marketing tips that you may find useful, especially if marketing is not part of your current job.

As the world becomes ever more connected through technology, the need to connect in meaningful ways has become increasingly important. Marketing for a library is about building community in this instantly changing, multichanneled world. Creating community sets the stage for great marketing impact.

If you are reading this book, you probably already know about all the captivating programs and engaging treasures in libraries. You are also probably well aware that there are scads of data that find a correlation between student academic success and library usage, and that it's important to bring people to the library when they are young and make them into lifelong users. Librarians don't need to be told that libraries offer tremendous programs, such as teaching digital literacy and STEM programs. But how do you get the message to your target audience, and how do you get them to act? It helps to nurture your community.

Following are some guidelines that you may find useful.

1. To build community, community members need to know that you are there.

Attention to the Message: Choose Great Photo Ops and Work Out in the Open
   Here's a story that illustrates how photo ops and publicity can help your cause.

In 2010 Gail Borden Public Library in Elgin, Illinois, headed up the local US Census campaign. This was not an effort that we had prepared for. It was nowhere to be found in our library's strategic plan. But a representative from our local foundation who had been very supportive of the library asked us to apply for a grant to motivate community members to return their census forms. Since the community had been undercounted in the previous census, we, like other libraries, considered the community need and agreed to take on this important challenge.

An author initiative has some sex appeal to the community and the media. People are intrigued by the authors who create compelling stories. The Census project was a different beast altogether. There weren't too many viral videos of cats playing with census forms. No reality TV plots evolved around whether people were sending in their forms. This was a hard environment to create message bounce, but the message was very important to our community. Every person who was counted would bring $2,500 in federal grants for the numerous projects that are supported by those grants.

We spent significant time trying to determine a photo op. Photos get your story read and quickly connect with people. According to graphic professional Mike Parkinson (2014), peoples' minds process photos 60,000 times faster than text. (There is a lot of compelling information about the power of graphics on this page, and Parkinson has also written the book *Do-It-Yourself Billion Dollar Graphics: 3 Fast and Easy Steps to Turn Your Text and Ideas into Persuasive Graphics*.) Interesting photos can elevate your coverage from page 15 to page 3 or even the front page.

It also helps to have dedicated, creative people on your team. We brought our group together and brainstormed for over an hour trying to come up with a compelling photo op for the census effort, dredging up ideas that would make paint dry even slower. Nothing was working.

The next day, the person who managed our copy center said, "I looked it up. If we make a form that is 20 by 30 feet, we will set the record for the largest government form." Who knew that the world's largest government form was a thing? It was.

Within days, the creative team had designed the world's largest census form. They printed it out in 20-foot-long strips. We carefully taped it together right in the middle of the library. We needed the room, and doing this let us talk to many people about the census, the need to mail the form back, and the upcoming kickoff event. It also garnered a story in the paper.

A few days later we invited everyone to the library's parking lot to unfurl the census form (see figure C.1). The mayor signed the form along with many others. The city's staff were active partners in the census effort. We asked the fire department to have a fire truck brought over (there were no fire calls during this time), and we brought some attention to the census effort. Partnerships were also crucial to this effort. What was the impact? There was a 78 percent census form return rate from our community, an 8 percent improvement from 2000.

Figure C.1. Although never entered for validation by world record-keeping bodies, we believe that this is the world's largest government census form, unfurled at the Gail Borden Public Library in Elgin, Illinois.

Pay attention to ideas from everyone.

What kind of photo ops can you come up with to build audience for your author awards initiative, or for your library in general? What images will grab attention? Does your contest have a special theme you can play up? Do some brainstorming, and see what you can come up with.

2. The press is still a vital member of your community.

Newspapers are dead, right? In reality, they are no more dead than Paul McCartney was dead during the *Abbey Road* album release. And in fact, he still is not dead, but actively contributing musically. Newspapers, or more accurately media companies, are not dead either. They are just transforming like we all are and, like Sir Paul, are still active contributors to their communities.

Many newspapers are affiliated with radio and television stations. Visit the *Wikipedia* page https://en.wikipedia.org/wiki/Media_cross-ownership _in_the_United_States, and it will have probably changed at least 1,000 times between my writing this and our publication date, but it gives you a sense of how much newspapers, television, and entertainment companies are intertwined. The connections are everywhere. Stories that start in the paper quickly move to social media, radio, and television. The sharing goes in every direction.

The first thing to consider when working with the press is a tip you should use with any relationship. Reporters are professional people just like you. They have families and professional ambitions. *Get to know them.* They amplify your message, whether you want them to or not. That is their job, and their job is more difficult than ever. Several years ago, their news beats were much smaller. Now they are the size of the state of Nebraska. Make it easy for them to cover you.

Here are some other tips you can use right away. These come from reporters themselves, so listen up:

- DO NOT just attach press releases to your emails. Reporters often check for releases on cell phones, and attachments don't work. Always embed the full text of your release in the email so they can access your message immediately.
- Be thoughtful about the timing of your events if you would like press coverage. In our community, the reporters said they were more likely to get a photographer assigned if the event happened during the week. Photographers cover a lot of sports on the weekends.
- They also talked about the format that they liked. One of our reporters really likes to cut and paste the date and time from releases, but she needs them in a certain format.

Also, remember to ask reporters whether they will run your photos. Sometimes they will. On the other hand, you may have some great professional photographers in your community. Often they will let you use their photos in your own publications if you use the "courtesy of" language. Reporters generally want good things for the communities they cover, and they are more than willing to communicate.

In 2014 Gail Borden Public Library ran an extremely complex geographic campaign to bring some unserved enclaves into our library district. There are swaths of Illinois that are not served by a library district. I cannot emphasize enough how complex this referendum effort was; the question had to win in both the unserved areas and the existing library district. We consulted with our attorneys often. Early on, one of our local reporters was writing a story. Because we had a good two-way relationship, the reporter called and told us that the votes would be tallied by the four precincts in the unserved area, not as a whole. We corrected our messaging. This complicated question did not pass, but we have had people join the library district as a result, and we made new connections in the unserved area.

Our other beat reporter has lived in our community for many years. Often she will mention potential partners for new projects. When we need to know something, she will call.

The bottom line is that it is great to nurture relationships with reporters. Make their job easier, and you'll undoubtedly see results.

3. Press releases inform the community.

The press release is still a mainstay of the marketing process. It is the who, what, why, when, where, and how information. It also needs to compete against every other press release that is coming to the reporter, who is covering a much larger territory these days.

Work on the angles. Being first, unique, or very important helps. Of course, answer the question about why people should care. If you can include contact information for people who can help flesh out the story, reporters seem to value that. And also check your work before sending: using correct spelling, grammar, and punctuation is fundamental.

Another thing worth mentioning is that the press release needs to be released. That seems perfectly obvious, but it is still worth mentioning. The release is art, and it can always be improved. Almost always, if you edit for days, improvements can be made. A good word can be made perfect or "perfecter." However, time matters in marketing, especially when you are asking for the reporters to do a preview piece. Taking a few extra days to make an "A" release into an "A+" can cost you a lot of audience. The closer you get to an event, the more you are risking that other news will knock your story out of coverage. If you can, send your release two weeks before your event. Then you can always follow up with another email or phone call. That way, if you are successful in getting news coverage, you can leverage that through all of your social media channels.

When you combine an engaging release with a photo op idea, the impact grows exponentially. Consider one of the campaigns we ran at our library.

A few years ago Gail Borden opened a drive-up window. We decided to use a non-PC, but effective, "Would You Like Fries with That?" campaign. Our director and deputy director were great sports, dressing up like car hops, handing out coupons for fries and coffee from our local McDonald's and dog treats for customers with canines riding in their cars (see figure C.2.). Our leaders served the cars for only about 45 minutes, but the story made pages one and three respectively in our local papers, and many people became aware of the library's new service.

Figure C.2. Gail Borden Executive Director Carole Medal and Deputy Director Karen Maki greet library drive-up window customers on opening day.

If you're looking for inspiration for your author awards press release, consider some of the Soon to be Famous press releases (and especially their lead-ins) below. These are examples from Gail Borden Public Library press releases written by Liz Clemmons (part of this book's editing team).

SOON TO BE FAMOUS PRESS RELEASE OPENINGS

Winner announced in 2015 Soon to be Famous Illinois Author Project

Michael Alan Peck has written about subjects ranging from TV to restaurants to travel, but on Thursday, April 16, he was honored with the 2015 Soon to be Famous Illinois Author Project award for his urban fantasy novel *The Commons Book 1: The Journeyman*. A Chicago resident, Peck accepted the award in a ceremony held at the ILA (Illinois Library Association) headquarters in Chicago.

ORIGINAL SOON TO BE FAMOUS PROJECT ANNOUNCEMENT

October 30, 2013

Undiscovered Author Needed by Illinois Libraries to Become Famous

Illinois libraries hope to discover an unknown self-published author whose work will jump off the page for readers. *The Soon to be Famous Illinois Author* project will be accepting adult fiction submissions from Illinois residents via their local libraries. The *Soon to be Famous Illinois Author* will be announced during National Library Week, April 13 to 19, 2014.

It is the perfect fit for Illinois libraries to discover an exciting work of fiction, as libraries have been a keystone in creating enthusiasm for reading for centuries. Even in this digital age, every day, library staff across the state of Illinois, recommend written works as well as host author talks and book clubs.

BALD EAGLES SIGHTED AT GAIL BORDEN LIBRARY IN ELGIN

Inside the library, children are learning how to be life-long readers while right outside, along the Fox River, young eaglets are learning how to fish to become lifelong hunters.

Although parents and their children have been visiting Gail Borden Library for more than 100 years, this is only the second year in a row that Bald Eagles with their families have been seen from the library. Last winter, several mature as well as young eagles were spotted along the river just north of the library for a little over a month.

ELGIN AL FRESCO—A TASTE OF THE ARTS

2012 Public Art Exhibit Wants to Entice Young Readers Along with Community Groups and Artists

ELGIN—This year's public art project is guaranteed to make *The Very Hungry Caterpillar* even hungrier, entice Sam, I Am to try *Green Eggs and Ham* and predict that this summer will be more fun than *Cloudy with a Chance of Meatballs*.

DISCOVERY 2012 SCIENCE EXPOSITION WILL TEST HYPOTHESIS: STUDENTS WHO SHOWCASE THEIR SCIENCE PROJECTS = STUDENTS WHO GET EXCITED ABOUT SCIENCE!

ELGIN—What do potatoes, popcorn and pickles have in common? They will be materials used by some plucky students when demonstrating their science projects at this Saturday's Discovery 2012 Science Exposition at Gail Borden Public Library, 270 N. Grove Ave.

JESSE WHITE TUMBLERS TO LAUNCH SUMMER READING CELEBRATION

Performances at Highland and Sheridan Elementary Schools October 17

ELGIN—Although Dist. U-46 and Gail Borden Public Library officials felt like jumping for joy when they heard the final numbers for children participating and finishing this year's summer reading program, they are willing to let the Jesse White Tumblers do the somersaults and handsprings.

DISCOVER THE PERSONAL STORIES OF WORLD WAR II VETERANS

Author Jeff Meek to discuss his book *They Answered the Call November 11*

ELGIN—Frank Covey of the 5th Marine Division spent his 20th birthday on Iwo Jima, eating "C" rations, repairing communication lines that the Japanese would sever to undermine U.S. Marines and trying to stay alive.

* * *

Gene Powell, Jr. of the U.S. Army's 45th Infantry Division traveled through Italy then over the Alps to Austria, into Germany and finally reaching a camp in Poland, where he was often guarded by fanatical SS troopers.

* * *

Reginald Brunson of the 20th Army Air Force flew B-29 bombers over Japan at night, sometimes returning to the base with just enough fuel to land.

GAIL BORDEN LIBRARY TO TRAVEL TO THE COUNTRY OF PANEM, ALL OF TIME AND SPACE, AND INFINITY AND BEYOND!

What do Katniss, Doctor Who, Buzz and Woody have in common? They will be the focus of fun programs at Gail Borden Library, 270 N. Grove Ave., Elgin, 60120, right before the Thanksgiving holiday in November.

CELEBRATE FANTASY AT GAIL BORDEN LIBRARY MAY 22

Kings, queens and Hobbits, wizards and vampires, urban heroes and mythical creatures have been gathered together in the Main Library's new Fantasy section at 270 N. Grove Ave., Elgin, IL 60120.

GAIL BORDEN LIBRARY INVITES COMMUNITY TO *READ ON THE WILD SIDE* THIS SUMMER

The largest croc to roam the earth ate dinosaurs, but readers will devour books instead this summer at Gail Borden Library, where the community will have an appetite for all things wild—participating in the *READ on the Wild Side* summer reading program and visiting the SuperCroc exhibit on display at the library.

Remember, a strong headline or lead-in makes all the difference. This is your chance to be creative.

4. Communities are made up of many partners—to start new great projects and rejuvenate older ones.

As you will note by the number of contributors to this book, the Soon to be Famous Illinois Author Project is based on partnerships between libraries. We can testify that the sum of this project is greater than its parts, and a whole lot more fun was had due to this fact.

To illustrate the power of partnerships, consider the following story about how we rejuvenated an established program through partnerships.

Our library district has been holding a summer reading program for over 50 years. Through those many years, it has been the library's summer reading program. Four years ago, by quite a stroke of luck, the past head of our youth department took a new position, the Director of Early Literacy and Learning Initiatives, and her new office was located near the exhibit/marketing department. Now our library hosts exhibits, and we partner with many organizations in the community—including the schools and the city—to maximize the exhibit's impact.

So two departments, and their respective staffs, that were previously separated by floors have much more contact, which creates many more opportunities to chat about processes. This dynamic led to a hypothetical question, namely: Why don't we talk to all of the exhibit partners about partnering on summer reading? The rest is history. Come to find out, every organization in the community cares about the reading skills of our children.

Marketing the summer reading program became everyone's mission. The summer reading program became a community summer reading program. Many remarkable things happened. Here are a few:

- The superintendent issued a school-district-wide challenge to the students.
- Local school principals used their robocalls to urge their students to sign up for the library's summer reading program.

- Some of the local schools used their outdoor signage to urge students to sign up for the library's summer reading program.
- The city provided the library with free pool passes to help motivate students to complete the summer reading program.
- The community carnivals provided free wristbands for reading finishers to ride as much as they wanted on a Thursday evening.
- The park district and the summer schools ran the summer reading program.
- The public art project switched its theme to match the library's summer reading theme.
- Local businesses named their specials after the library's summer reading theme.

And what happened when the library's summer reading theme became exponentially partnered and became the community's summer reading program? The number of young people who finished the reading program doubled in one year, each additional number representing one child who had a better chance for future academic success. The numbers have continued to increase.

What can partnerships do for your author initiative? If you have read chapter 3, you hopefully have some ideas about that already. But consider specifically how your partners can help promote your project.

5. Creating community impact is about telling human stories.

The power of story—stories about people—is well known. Consider how you might employ this power in your author event initiative.

Following up on the summer reading story above, I would like to relate how the summer reading project won an Illinois Hometown Governor's Award (see figure C.3). To win this recognition, we had to travel to Springfield with some wonderful community members to make a presentation about our project's impact. We adult folks talked about all the wonderful things that happened.

But a high school junior was the person "who crushed it" in Springfield. Trevon Flowers, a high school junior, told the judges in Springfield about how the library was a home away from home for him and his siblings. Trevon told the judges how he brought his younger sisters and brothers to the library at least three times a week in the summer. He related how the carnival rides motivated his little brother to read even though he did not initially like reading. He talked about the joy that his young sisters experienced when they read and how they loved the games on the reading logs.

Figure C.3. The first Hometown Governor's Award presentation team in 2012. Left to right: Trevon Flowers (personal testimony), Denise Raleigh (representing library), Karen Fox (volunteer retired from School District U-46), and Steve Johnson (U-46 principal from Highland Elementary School).

Trevon's first-person story made all the difference to our entry. By the way, we are so proud that Trevon plans to attend Morehouse this fall. Thank-you, Trevon, for using the library and telling your story.

Do your finalists or winning authors have interesting ties to your community or experiences that set them apart? What was the impetus for their writing? Do some research and use it to create an angle for your story.

6. Your community is online.

Discussing using social media for library marketing and promotion could take a book in itself. However, it does warrant your attention in the context of your author awards initiative. Consider how social media helped our promotions.

Several members of our library recently attended a great presentation by Stephanie Moritz, senior director of PR, social media, and experimental marketing at ConAgra Foods, and we are going to modify some of what ConAgra's social media team practices and try out these techniques in our library. Moritz talked about social media listening and real-time marketing. She also shared a wonderful photo, "The Original

Social Media Explained with Donuts by Douglas Wray" (https://instagram.com/p/nm695/), which is well worth viewing. ConAgra owns over 30 food brands, including Chef Boyardee, Swiss Miss, and Marie Callender's, and has a social media team that meets twice daily to identify opportunities to engage.

We found out that the ConAgra customer's schedule—the family schedule—is also the basic schedule of many of our library customers. So in the coming year, we will be preparing graphics and posts that hopefully alert our customers about what the library has to offer in step with our library customers' schedules, posting and interacting when students enter school, when there are finals, and during vacations.

A number of staff members will meet briefly once a week to talk about what is in the news locally and nationally so that we can join conversations with increased relevance. Instead of starting with marketing library resources, we hope to make library resources more visible when customers will be the most interested.

The Soon to be Famous Facebook page has been a mainstay of the project. When the project was honored with the John Cotton Dana Award in San Francisco, the first place that photos appeared to further validate the project's value was on its Facebook page. The Reaching Across Illinois Library System's eNewsletter communication linked to the Facebook page within hours, pushing this great news out quickly. (See figure C.4.)

Figure C.4. Most of the Soon to be Famous Illinois Author contributors were able to attend the John Cotton Dana Awards at the American Library Annual Association Conference in 2015. From left to right: Nicole Zimmermann, Julie Stam, Denise Raleigh, Lucy Tarabour, Cris Cigler, Donna Fletcher, Sue Wilsey, Bob Doyle, and Dee Brennan.

Try to share media across channels. For example, we will run a video on our local television channel and on our YouTube channel and also push it out with our electronic newsletter. Photos we share on Flickr will also be shared through Twitter, Facebook, and the library's electronic newsletter.

7. Take time to assess.

Sometimes you are so busy marketing that you forget to assess. But to maximize message impact, you need to do that piece.

For instance, our library has been communicating through video for a decade. Thanks to our partners at the city, we also have a unique opportunity to use video on local public television. So we produce video about upcoming library programs, new services, and local historical interviews. However, when we checked our most watched video of 2014, it was an under two-minute time lapse of building a LEGO™ tower (https://www.youtube.com/watch?v=A4dlfiVX-Uo). Granted, it was a 20-foot-tall LEGO™ tower of the Burj Khalifa, built by LEGO™ architect Adam Reed Tucker, but it was not serious in any way. We determined that our customers like fun, quick, and behind-the-scenes videos. So now we mix in more of "the making of" in our videos, and they all get watched a little more.

Social media make it easy to check statistics. Attendance at programs can indicate whether your community received the message. We tweak continually to try to maximize marketing. Everything can always improve, and tools are constantly changing.

CONCLUSION

If you remember one tip, let it be this: the people and the resources in your library do great things. Do not be shy about letting others know. Be loud and proud about how your library makes a difference in your community.

REFERENCE

Parkinson, Mike. (2014). The power of visual communication. Retrieved from http://www.billiondollargraphics.com/infographics.html

RESOURCES FOR LIBRARY MARKETING
Print Resources

Bizzle, Ben, with Maria Flora. *Start a Revolution: Stop Acting Like a Library*. Chicago: ALA Editions, 2015.
Discusses cutting-edge library marketing. Topics include using Web sites, social media, campaigns, and messaging.

Crawford, Walt. *The Librarian's Guide to MicroPublishing: Helping Patrons and Communities Use Free and Low-Cost Publishing Tools to Tell Their Stories.* Medford, NJ: Information Today, Inc., 2012.

Discusses low-cost and no-cost publishing tools like Lulu and CreateSpace. Topics include templates, typography, layout, copyright, marketing, and other aspects of publishing books.

Dempsey, Kathy. *The Accidental Library Marketer.* Medford, NJ: Information Today, Inc., 2009.

Discusses various aspects of marketing in a library setting. Topics include communication, assessment, administrative buy-in, statistics, the marketing cycle, marketing plans, messaging, public relations, and outreach.

Doucett, Elisabeth. *Creating Your Library Brand: Communicating Your Relevance and Value to Your Patrons.* Chicago: American Library Association, 2008.

Discusses communicating relevance to stakeholders through branding. Topics include marketing and branding, setting goals, and defining your message.

Dowd, Nancy, Mary Evangeliste, and Jonathan Silberman. *Bite-Sized Marketing: Realistic Solutions for the Overworked Librarian.* Chicago: American Library Association, 2010.

Discusses contemporary marketing ideas. Topics include word-of-mouth marketing, telling your story, marketing electronic resources, public relations, outreach, advocacy, branding, marketing tools, and marketing best practices.

Fisher, Patricia H., and Marseille M. Pride. *Blueprint for Your Library Marketing Plan: A Guide to Help You Survive and Thrive.* Chicago: American Library Association, 2006.

Discusses creation and implementation of marketing plans. Topics include mining data, situation assessment, target markets, setting goals and objectives, promotion, plan creation, and implementation and assessment.

Potter, Ned. *The Library Marketing Toolkit.* London: Facet Publishing, 2012.

Provides a comprehensive overview of library marketing. Topics include strategic marketing, branding, online marketing, social media, internal marketing, and advocacy.

Siess, Judith A. *The Visible Librarian: Asserting Your Value with Marketing and Advocacy.* Chicago: American Library Association, 2003.

Discusses best practices in library marketing. Topics include customer service, marketing, publicity, public relations, and advocacy.

Smallwood, Carol, Vera Gubnitskaia, and Kerol Harrod (Eds.). *Marketing Your Library: Tips and Tools That Work.* Jefferson, NC: McFarland & Company, Inc., 2012.

Discusses effective marketing tools for libraries. Topics include brand management, campaign organization, community outreach, media interactions, social media, and event planning.

Walter, Ekaterina, and Jessica Gioglio. *The Power of Visual Storytelling: How to Use Visuals, Videos, and Social Media to Market Your Brand.* New York: McGraw-Hill Education, 2014.

Discusses how to leverage your ideas and your marketing campaigns through pictures, videos, infographics, and displays. Topics include marketing, promoting your brand, and telling your story through visual media.

Watson-Lakamp, Paula. *Marketing Moxie for Librarians: Fresh Ideas, Proven Techniques, and Innovative Approaches*. Santa Barbara, CA: Libraries Unlimited, 2015.

Online Resources

- The Library Marketing Toolkit: http://www.librarymarketingtoolkit.com/. A Web site full of stuff to help you market your library.
- The "M" Word—Marketing Libraries: http://themwordblog.blogspot.com/. Marketing tips and trends for libraries and nonprofits.
- Marketing Matters for Librarians: https://alisonwallbutton.wordpress.com/
- 658.8—Practical Marketing for Public Libraries: http://658point8.com/
- Fantastic library promotion ideas: https://www.pinterest.com/sjrcexchange/fantastic -library-promotion-ideas/
- Facebook groups (some are closed groups but welcoming to those working in libraries)

  Library Marketing and Outreach: https://www.facebook.com/groups/740944219 278343/

  Libraries Are Essential: https://www.facebook.com/LibrariesAreEssential?fref=nf

  ALA Think Tank: https://www.facebook.com/groups/ALAthinkTANK/?fref=nf

  Libraries and Social Media: https://www.facebook.com/groups/LibrarySocial/

  Geek the Library: https://www.facebook.com/geekthelibrary
- Twitter: Search "Library Marketing" and get a list of marketing people from every large publishing house. Also, many national library marketing superstars post frequently on Twitter. Here are favorites to follow:

  Ben Bizzle @LibraryMarket1
  Ned Potter @ned_potter
  ALA Advocacy @ILoveLibraries
  James LaRue @jaslar]
  David Lee King @davidleeking
  Stephen Abram @sabram
  Steven M. Cohen @LibraryStuff
  Rita Meade @ScrewyDecimal
  R. David Lankes @rdlankes
  Jeff Bullas @jeffbullas

Appendix D

CREATING A MARKETING PLAN FOR YOUR AUTHOR CONTEST

Christine Niels Cigler

Creating any marketing plan starts with setting a goal and identifying a target audience. Creating a marketing plan for an author contest entails identifying and targeting two completely separate goals and audiences, which in effect means you have to create two marketing plans: one for authors and one for librarians. Every marketing plan should include the following steps:

- Determine the goal.
- Identify the target audience.
- Conduct research.
- Develop strategies.
- Evaluate the results.

DETERMINE THE GOAL

The goal of marketing the contest to librarians is to engage them in the effort so that they can support it, promote it in their libraries, funnel applications to you, and act as judges, while the goal of marketing the contest to authors is for them to submit their works to the contest.

IDENTIFY THE TARGET AUDIENCE

The audience is local libraries and librarians and self-published authors.

CONDUCT RESEARCH

Find out how to best reach your target audience and what messages they will find relatable. For your librarians, you may consider starting with local, regional, or state library associations to see if the issues of self-publishing or eBooks are being discussed. Can you link to those trends?

Where can you find your audience? Are there listservs, networking groups, special interest groups, associations, conferences, meetings, or special events that would give you a platform for getting the word out? Try reaching out to authors through research writers' groups (many libraries have them), classes in creative writing, local colleges, and even local successful authors.

DEVELOP STRATEGIES

Is your audience responsive to materials in print? Electronically? Personally? Consider how you can use the following strategies:

- Internal marketing
- Word-of-mouth marketing
- Advertising
- Outreach
- Promotions
- Publicity
- Events
- Mailings
- Press releases
- Web site updates
- Electronic newsletters
- Social media

Make sure you create an easy-to-use guide for both librarians and authors that spells out all the details clearly and concisely. Once you've nailed that, you will have a consistent message that you can use in any number of ways. Make it easy for your audience to get all the information they need. Put yourself in their shoes and review your materials to see if all the questions are answered. Do not make authors or librarians search for the answers.

EVALUATE THE RESULTS

Finally, build in a step for evaluation. When you're working with your libraries and authors, find out how they heard about the project. This step will help you determine what worked and what didn't.

Remember: finding out that one of your strategies was ineffective is not failure. It is success because you have identified something that doesn't work. You will not waste time doing it again.

Appendix E

A SHORT HISTORY OF SELF-PUBLISHING

Elizabeth Clemmons

At first glance, it seems that authors have just started using self-publishing as a way to get their books to readers. Self-publishing has experienced explosive growth over the last 20 years and garnered much recent media attention. But authors taking matters into their own hands and bypassing traditional publishing has been occurring for a long time. Mark Twain, Virginia Woolf, Willa Cather, Beatrix Potter, and Margaret Atwood (Dilevko & Dali, 2006) are just some of the famous authors who at one time self-published their work.

Another author who took the nontraditional route was Irma Rombauer, author of *The Joy of Cooking*. In 1931 Rombauer paid a local printing company to print 3,000 copies of her cookbooks at $1 each. A large printing house took over five years later. The book has been printed continuously ever since, with more than 18 million copies sold (Balson, 2013).

A more recent example of successful self-publishing is the beginning of the Fifty Shades trilogy. Author E. L. James published *Fifty Shades of Grey* as an eBook, and it caught on via Facebook and word of mouth (Fay, 2012). Eventually, James procured a seven-figure book deal with a major publisher and sold movie rights to the book.

For many years, self-publishing was referred to as "vanity publishing" and had a reputation for representing low-quality books not good enough to be published by major publishers. Then came desktop publishing in the 1980s, which attracted writers who wanted to be self-published. The Internet followed, as did eBooks (Milliot, 2010). Technology transformed the self-publishing industry, making it cheaper and more accessible to get books out there via print on demand offerings and eReaders. Self-publishing companies simplified the process of getting a book published but also offered authors more control over how their books were edited, how they looked, and how they were marketed (Glazer, 2005).

Self-publishing continues to increase. According to an author earnings report from 2014 about Amazon's top-selling titles, the Big Five traditional publishers account for only 16 percent of eBooks on Amazon's best-seller list; self-published books represent 31 percent of eBook sales from the Kindle store; and indie authors take in nearly 40 percent of eBook author earnings (Sargent, 2014).

Some of today's most popular self-publishing platforms are Amazon's Kindle Direct Publishing, NOOK Press, Kobo Writing Life, Smashwords, CreateSpace, and Lulu. These offer eBook publishing, print on demand capabilities, and author services such as editing and cover design for extra costs. These platforms often offer package deals for services.

What's ahead for self-publishing? Among the near-future changes: self-published authors will continue to become more business savvy, traditional publishing and self-publishing will sometimes work together for the benefit of both, and authors served by traditional publishers will sometimes find it beneficial to turn to self-publishing (McCartney, 2015). No matter how it evolves, the story of self-publishing continues!

REFERENCES

Balson, Ronald H. (2013, October 8). *Bestseller success stories that started out as self-published books* (blog). *Huffington Post.* Retrieved from http://www.huffingtonpost.com /ronald-h-balson/bestseller-success-storie_b_4064574.html

Dilevko, Juris, & Dali, Keren. (2006). The self-publishing phenomenon and libraries. *Library & Information Science Research, 28*(2), 209. Retrieved from http://www .moyak.com/papers/self-publishing.pdf

Fay, Sarah. (2012, April 2). After "Fifty Shades of Grey," what's next for self-publishing? *The Atlantic.* Retrieved from http://www.theatlantic.com/entertainment/archive/2012/04 /after-fifty-shades-of-grey-whats-next-for-self-publishing/255338/

Glazer, Sarah. (2005, April 24). How to be your own publisher. *The New York Times Sunday Book Review.* Retrieved from http://www.nytimes.com/2005/04/24/books/review /how-to-be-your-own-publisher.html?_r=0

McCartney, Jennifer. (2015, January 16). A look ahead to self-publishing in 2015. *Publishers Weekly.* Retrieved from http://www.publishersweekly.com/pw/by-topic/authors /pw-select/article/65299-a-look-ahead-to-self-publishing-in-2015.html

Milliot, Jim, & Coffey, Michael. (2010, December 10). PW select: Self publishing comes of age. *Publishers Weekly, 257*(50), 1. Retrieved from http://www.publishersweekly .com/pw/print/20101220/45558-pw-select-self-publishing-comes-of-age.html

Sargent, Betty Kelly. (2014, July 28). Surprising self-publishing statistics. *Publishers Weekly.* Retrieved from http://www.publishersweekly.com/pw/by-topic/authors/pw -select/article/63455-surprising-self-publishing-statistics.html

Appendix F

THE FIRST SOON TO BE FAMOUS ILLINOIS AUTHOR— THE MOVIE

Joanne Zienty

When Hollywood makes the movie version, it will star Julia Roberts. Or maybe Demi Moore, in her comeback role for which she will finally win an Oscar for Best Actress.

The first twenty minutes will, of course, reveal our heroine in her ordinary world: going for her morning run through the park, teaching the difference between fiction and nonfiction to a class of rambunctious first graders, trouble-shooting computer problems for a technology-challenged colleague, listening to the classical music station on her drive home, preparing her favorite shrimp dish for dinner while she drinks a glass of wine, reading the morning papers in the evening, falling asleep with a book in her hand, and getting up in the morning to do it all again. And maybe squeezing in a little writing here and there.

Then comes the pivotal "call to adventure" scene. The busy Christmas holidays are over; New Year's Eve has come and gone. The camera, shooting through the window, captures the snowflakes falling over already snow-packed ground as the sky darkens toward evening. Camera cuts to the kitchen again. We hear the audio of a newscast coming from the living room. It's the weather report, warning of accumulating and blowing snow, plummeting temperatures and dangerously cold wind chills. A second voice intones that school districts across the region will be closed the following day.

Amidst the seasonal bustle, several days' worth of newspapers have piled up on the counter. Our heroine gathers them up to toss in the recycling bin, when an article catches her eye. The camera zooms in on the headline in its stark, bold font: **Illinois library contest aimed at changing e-book policies**. The camera pans down the newspaper, catching significant phrases along the way:

"Soon to be Famous Illinois Author Project will choose a self-published Illinois author's work. . . ."

". . . bringing acclaim to one writer laboring in obscurity. . . ."

". . . submissions will be accepted until January 6. . . ."

The camera jump cuts from the newspaper to our heroine's face, her eyes afire. Then it follows her gaze to her Librarian's Desk Calendar from Upstart. It zooms in again, this time on the date: January 5th.

Our heroine utters a clipped expletive and bursts into action. The camera follows her frenzied fingers as they tap out the contest site's URL in the address box of her web browser and closes in on her lips as they utter another curse waiting for the page to load. There's a close-up of the entry submission form. Cut to our heroine's face, worry etched across her forehead. One day left . . . fade out.

Fade in. Interior: bathroom—morning. Our heroine stands in front of her mirror, brushing her hair. The state of her hair is very important to our heroine's confidence level. This morning it's looking good. The camera draws in for a close-up. Her face is determined, her eyes resolute.

The camera follows her down the staircase to the foyer. She zips up her black winter coat. She eyes the knit hat that she only wears while shoveling snow. No, she will go hatless into the polar vortex, braving wind chills of 40° below zero. *(Because it's all about the hair.)* The camera pans to the kitchen counter, where a book sits, waiting. A close-up on our heroine's hand as she scoops it up and hugs it close.

A montage of driving scenes under a brilliant sky the color of hope. The sun is blinding, reflecting off the new snow, which winks diamonds in our heroine's path, but it holds not even the merest breath of warmth. We hear the crunch of the car tires as they roll over the neighborhood streets crusted with ice and frozen slush. The camera follows the old silver Accord as it turns into the parking lot of our heroine's local public library.

The camera cuts to our heroine's face as she climbs out of the car. The white plumes of her breath are in stark contrast to her scarlet lips and black coat. But she doesn't notice the extreme chill, because her intense focus on completing her mission has lit a fire within.

The camera adopts our heroine's viewpoint as she strides through the sliding doors and up to the circulation desk, where a smiling woman looks up.

Smiling woman
Yes? Can I help you?

Our heroine
I'm a local author. I live here in town. And I'd like to have the
library nominate my book for the Soon to be Famous Illinois

Author Project. *(Places her novel on the counter.)* You actually already have a copy in the library, but I also brought—

Smiling woman
Oh, the person that is handling that for the library is out sick today. *(Squints at a laminated piece of paper on the desk.)* And she's not scheduled to work tomorrow either. I can give you her name and number. *(Writes on and hands over a green Post-It Note.)*

Close-up on our heroine's face as her determination slowly gives way to resignation as she realizes that she's not going to make the deadline.

Our heroine
(crestfallen, but polite) Thank-you.

Cut to an exterior shot, in the parking lot. Our heroine leans back against her car, discouragement hanging heavily at the corners of her eyes and lips. As she heaves a sigh, her ghost-white breath envelopes her face. She suddenly becomes aware of the frigid air, as the tears freeze on her lashes. She pulls up the hood of her coat, her head disappearing into its black void, because the hair doesn't matter anymore. . . . Fade out.

Fade in. Interior: family room—afternoon. Our heroine slumps in her ergonomic desk chair in front of her computer hutch. But as the camera closes in, we can see that her mind is racing.

Our heroine (in voice-over)
All right, keep it together. Stay calm. There's got to be a way. Who else can I ask? There are other librarians that I know . . . but it's so last minute. . . .

A wide shot. We can see her running through her mental Rolodex, her foot jiggling, fingers tapping restlessly on the leatherette arm of the chair. Then the tapping abruptly stops; both feet come to rest on the wooden floor. The camera eases in to catch the light that's slowly dawning in her eyes. (If this was a cartoon, the clichéd light-bulb would be blinking over her head.)

Our heroine (in voice-over)
Wait a second. I don't need to find another librarian to nominate my book. I don't need to find another librarian because—
(rising from her chair, saying aloud) I AM a librarian!

The music swells. Montage of our heroine filling out the entry form, typing the email, attaching the file, clicking the send button. Fade out.

The ensuing section of the movie portrays the classic "road of trials" that all heroes must endure. We see our heroine moving through her day-to-day life, anxiously checking her email. The camera captures her joy when her novel is accepted into the contest. It watches as she hastily sends off multiple MOBI e-book files to the readers for the first round of judging. Luckily, she already has an account with Smashwords to facilitate this. However, we also see her fraught with anxiety when a couple of judges are unable to open the file, so she has to quickly send them links for gift copies from Amazon that will work on their Kindles. The bitterly cold winter drags on.

The camera zooms in on the Librarian's Desk Calendar. It's February. The camera cuts to our heroine's face. She's perched again in front of her computer, perusing her email. The light from its monitor casts a bluish glow over her skin. Tight close-up on her smile; then camera cuts to the monitor, where we see the words of the email:

Congratulations! Your book has been selected to move to the second round of the Soon to be Famous Illinois Author project. The 15 titles selected for the second round are now listed at www.soontobefamous.info.

Music swells. Montage of exterior scenes of mounds of dirty snow beginning to shrink. Camera zooms in yet again on the desk calendar *(Producer's note: consider product placement royalty from Upstart.)* It's March. The text of another email scrolls over the scene:

Congratulations! You have advanced to the final round of the Soon to be Famous Illinois Author Project.

But there is one last trial for our heroine to endure: the telephone interview with the anonymous voices of "The Committee." The camera keeps a medium shot as she sits behind her desk in her school library, phone clutched to her ear.

Our heroine

Well, of course, I'd be happy to travel around to Illinois libraries promoting my book. . . . *(listening, nodding)* Yes, I am pretty comfortable speaking in front of people, I am a teacher, after all, so I'm accustomed to it. . . . You need a head shot? Cool beans!

(Camera zooms in to our heroine's face.)

It'll give me an excuse to go to the salon and get my hair done!

Music swells. The classic makeover montage to the sound of Katy Perry's "Roar." *(Producer's note: get permission rights, maybe a cameo by Katy?)* Ends with a beautiful, author-type head shot.

Close-up of Librarian Desk Calendar. It's April. A banner caption comes spinning forward: *National Book Week. (Producer's note: this would be a fabulous effect in 3-D.)* Cut to our heroine sitting in her Accord outside of an unfamiliar, low-slung building. The day is warm, bright and windy. Camera zooms in. We can see she is anxious. Her hair is looking a little wind-blown. But she heaves a sigh, puts on her game face and exits the vehicle.

Our heroine (in voice-over)
(walking) It's an honor just to make the top three. You know they will pick one of the other authors because mysteries and chick-lit are just easier to promote than literary fiction, especially dark, literary fiction . . . (chewing her lip). Maybe they couldn't decide and they will pick all three of us. No, face it, you are going to lose. But it's not a loss because it's an honor just to make the top three. . . .

Jump-cut to the three authors sitting in front of a crowded room full of librarians who are wearing stylish clothes and sensible shoes. The other two don't seem particularly nervous, but our heroine feels the wings of anxiety fluttering inside her stomach.

Our heroine (in voice-over)
(head craned to listen to the speaker) Wow, this must be how the actors feel at the Academy Awards.

The tall, dark, and "brandsome" stranger from New York, veteran of Coke and car ad campaigns, says nice things about all three authors. The camera focuses on each as they get up to give brief remarks in turn. Our heroine goes last, because, of course, these things are done in alphabetical order. She's used to it.

Our heroine
Think of the authors and their treasures that we may not have read if they were attempting to publish today, writers of difficult books that require a great investment of time and concentration in this instant gratification world. Melville comes to mind.

And Tolstoy, whose query e-mail would have been immediately deleted from an agent's inbox because nobody reads a pitch for novel with a word count over 100,000, much less 600,000. And Hawthorne. For goodness sake, he wrote a book about adultery without the sex parts! I mean, in this *Fifty Shades of Grey* world, would *The Scarlet Letter* see the light of day?

(tearing up a little, struggling to get the words out) Full many a flower may be born to blush unseen, but I think libraries' next mission may be to find those blossoms that deserve to join the bouquet. . . .

Camera pans wide angle as our heroine returns to her seat.

Our heroine (in voice-over)
Cry baby. . . that was really stupid. . . now when you don't win,
you'll look like a blubbering idiot. . . .

The tall, dark and brandsome stranger makes a brief remark about this being an end, but more importantly, a beginning. Camera focuses in on our heroine, who at this point is obviously just praying for it to all be over. And yet, still, in her mind:

Our heroine (in voice-over)
Let him say my name. . . .

And then he speaks. And the world goes very quiet for a few split seconds as our heroine realizes that he has.
And she wishes she'd brushed her hair.

REFERENCE

This excerpt from the author's Soon to be Famous award ceremony speech was previously printed in "Illinois' First Soon to Be Famous Author," *The ILA* [Illinois Library Association] *Reporter* 32, no. 3 (June 2014): 14–15.

INDEX

Adamowski, Betsy, 31
ALA Office for Information Technology Policy, 25
American Library Association (ALA), 1, 7, 11, 24, 29
Amling, Jennifer, 17, 34 (photo)
announcement of the winning author: location, 50, 68–69; marketing of, 69–70; planning the ceremony, 50, 70–72; press releases, 50, 78
Anthony, Carolyn, 26
author awards project: creating a marketing plan, 127–128; creating video for, 20–21; creating Web site for, 17–19; evaluating the outcome, 87–92; questions from authors, 6; timeline, 49, 95–96
authors: communicating with, 35–36, 49, 67–68; getting books from, 44–45; submissions, 35–36

Barrington Public Library, 20
Bednar, Leslie, 24, 31
Bertrand, Steve, 77 (photo)
Berwyn Public Library, 75
Big Five (publishers), 1, 3, 4, 90, 91, 129
Big Question podcast, 80
Booklist Online, 88
books: eBooks versus paper, 41–42; nomination form, 99–101; sales of author award winner, 88–89; writing a review, 109–110
Brennan, Dee, 20, 23, 24, 69, 123 (photo)

Calhamer, Tish, 75 (photo)
Change of Address, 51
Chicago Public Library, 24
Chicago Tribune, 7, 20, 21, 28, 37, 88
Cigler, Christine Niels (Cris), 11, 32 (photo) 33 (photo), 34 (photo), 123 (photo)

Clarendon Hills Public Library, 34
Clark, Larra, 25
Clemmons, Elizabeth (Liz), 29, 33 (photo), 116
The Commons Book 1: The Journeyman, 51, 61, 93, 117
ConAgra Foods, 122, 123
Crump, Amy, 31

Daily Herald, 8, 28, 88
Digital Content Working Group, 7, 24, 25
The Digital Reader, 89
Dilger, Jeannie, 74
Donna E. Fletcher Consulting, Inc., 33
Doyle, Robert (Bob), 20, 23, 25, 31, 123 (photo)
Dundee Public Library, 78

Eisenhower Public Library District, 27, 33
.EPUB file, 19, 37, 43, 44, 45, 99, 101, 102
Espinoza, Laura, 32

Fletcher, Donna, 33 (photo), 34 (photo), 35, 123 (photo)
Flowers, Trevon, 122
Forbes, 11, 28, 69, 88
Fox, Karen, 122
Free Library of Philadelphia (FLP), 5

Gail Borden Public Library, 27, 31, 33, 75, 79, 80, 112, 113, 115, 116
Gardner, Melissa, 31
genres, 4, 14–15, 38, 103, 105, 109
Green, Samuel, 3
Gutenberg, Johannes, 2
Gutenberg press, 4

Helen Plum Memorial Library, 34
Highland Elementary School, 122

Highland Park Public Library, 33
Hilyard, Nann Blaine, 31
Hoffelder, Nate, 89
Hometown Governor's Award, 122
Hopkins, Elizabeth, 75 (photo)
The House of Closed Doors, 51

ILA Reporter, 88
Illinois Heartland Library System, 7, 16,
    24, 30, 31
Illinois Library Association (ILA):
    promoting STBF at the ILA
    Conference, 29, 30, 31, 74;
    supporting STBF, 7, 8, 11–16, 12,
    21, 24, 26–27, 37, 69, 71, 77, 93, 95
Illinois Library Association (ILA)
    Marketing Committee, 11, 21
Indian Prairie Public Library, 14, 20, 33
It's a Writingful Life, 2, 30, 31, 32

John Cotton Dana Award, 93, 123
Johnson, Steve, 122
Judges: at 2014 Soon to be Famous
    announcement, 75 (photo); avoiding
    conflicts of interest, 43, 97; getting
    books to, 36–37, 42–43, 45;
    instructions on downloading books,
    102; recruitment form, 97–98
Judging: first round, 46–47; first-round
    judging form, 104; first-round
    judging guidelines, 103; process, 44;
    reviewing guidelines, 105; rubric, 48,
    49, 107; second round, 47–48; third
    round, 48–49

Kay, Sharon, 51
Keefe, Karen Kleckner, 31

La Grange Public Library, 33, 74
librarians: involved in author awards
    program, 15; involvement in *It's
    a Writingful Life*, 2; promoting an
    author awards program, 15–16, 17,
    127–128; questions about an author
    awards program, 38–39; recruiting as
    judges, 28, 43–44; supporting indie
    authors, 73–75, 88

libraries: as educational hubs, 5–6; future
    roles in author awards programs, 88;
    hosting a winning author, 76–77,
    79; influencing readers, 73–74,
    93; involvement in STBF, 15, 36,
    87, 89–90; marketing guidelines,
    111–124; marketing resources,
    124–126; marketing the winning
    author, 69–70, 78, 80, 81; submitting
    nominations, 37–40; nonsubmitting,
    39–40; offering self-published books,
    5; partnering with local authors, 7,
    26; partnering with publishers, 1, 90,
    93; promoting works of authors, 24;
    promoting reading and literature, 25;
    providing books, 2–4; purchasing
    The Things We Save, 88; staying
    relevant, 4–5; value of, 12
Library Discover Project, 93
Library Journal, 5, 50, 88
Library Services and Technology Act
    (LSTA), 93
Lisle Library District, 75
Lyons, Karen Danczak, 31

Maki, Karen, 116 (photo)
Mannion, Annemarie, 7
McBride, Karen, 20, 29, 32 (photo)
Medal, Carole, 31, 116
.MOBI Kindle file, 19, 37, 43, 44, 45, 99,
    101, 102
Moritz, Stephanie, 122

National Library Week, 16, 29, 33, 50,
    68, 70
Niles Public Library, 33
Nominations, tracking of, 36
Northwestern Medicine Central DuPage
    Hospital, 75

Online Computer Library Center (OCLC),
    3, 4

Papaurelis, Theresa, 14
Pearson, Lynnanne, 75 (photo)
Peck, Michael Alan, 51, 61, 93, 117
Pitchford, Veronda, 29

Plainfield Public Library, 33
Polad, Rick, 51
Polar Vortex, 21, 33, 37
promoting the winning author: groups, 17,
    77–78; press kit, 78; print media, 81;
    social media, 81; word of mouth, 79;
    Web site, 17–19, 80
Public Library Association (PLA), 7, 16,
    24, 26
Publishers Weekly, 3, 50

Quinlan, Anita, 33 (photo), 34 (photo), 67

RAILS Marketing Group, 11, 21
Raleigh, Denise, 1, 23, 30 (photo),
    33 (photo), 34 (photo), 111, 122
    (photo), 123 (photo)
Ranganathan, S. R., 3, 4, 5
Reaching Across Illinois Library System
    (RAILS): assisting with STBF
    winner announcement event, 68,
    69, 70–71; partnering with, 16, 77;
    promoting STBF, 77, 123; supporting
    STBF, 7, 8, 11, 21, 23, 24, 26, 27,
    69, 95
Reed, Mary Hutchings, 51
rubric for judging books, 48–49, 107

St. Charles Public Library, 75
Schiltz, Marlise, 75 (photo)
School Library Journal, 88
self-published books: accepted by
    libraries, 5; determination of, 47;
    promoting, 89–90; statistics on,
    3–4, 5
self-publishing: changing attitudes
    toward, 73–75; determination of
    books, 47; short history, 129–130
Skokie Public Library, 75
social media, 12, 17, 70, 79, 81, 114, 115,
    122, 123
Soon to be Famous Illinois Author
    Project (STBF): announcement

event, 50, 67–72; bookmarks, 27
    (photo); committee, 6; forming a
    team, 11–13; helping readers find
    books, 4–5, 7; John Cotton Dana
    Award, 93; judges, 7; logo, 14
    (photo); movie, 131–136; naming of,
    13; nominations, 35–38; partnering
    with publishers, 90, 93; PR effect,
    37; promoting the winner, 78–81;
    promotion of, 29; sales of winning
    book, 88–89; self-published authors,
    40, 51; sponsorship, 81; timeline,
    21, 95–96; Web site, 17–19, 26
    (photo)
Spratford, Becky, 75 (photo)
Stam, Julianne (Julie), 27 (photo), 30
    (photo), 33 (photo), 34 (photo), 41,
    123 (photo)
Steen, Jane, 51
Stielstra, Julie, 75 (photo)

Tarabour, Lucy, 34 (photo), 87, 93, 123
    (photo)
The Things We Save, 8, 37, 51, 52, 88

Vinjamuri, David, xiv, 1, 3, 11, 21, 25, 28,
    29, 47, 50, 69, 70, 75

WDCB Radio, 88
WGN Radio, 77, 88
Warming Up, 51
Weiss, Linda, 31
Wheaton Public Library, 76
Wicked Waves, 51
Wilsey, Sue, 33 (photo), 34 (photo), 123
    (photo)
Worldcat, 88

Zienty, Joanne, 18, 37, 51, 52, 72, 76
    (photo), 77 (photo), 79 (photo), 81,
    88, 91, 131
Zimmerman, Nicole (Nikki), 29, 33
    (photo), 34 (photo), 73, 123

About the Editors and Contributors

EDITORS

JULIANNE STAM is the marketing specialist at Eisenhower Public Library District in Harwood Heights, Illinois. Julie is a member of the Illinois Library Association Marketing Committee, the RAILS Marketing Group, and a founding member of the Soon to be Famous Illinois Author Project (STBF). For the STBF committee, Julie was tasked with handling the judging process for selecting a winning author. Julie has presented programs at the American Library Association and Internet Librarian conferences. She received her BS in marketing and MBA in marketing research from DePaul University, and her MLIS from Drexel University's iSchool. Julie can be reached at juliestam67@gmail.com.

ELIZABETH CLEMMONS is the public relations coordinator at Gail Borden Public Library in Elgin, Illinois. She is a member of the RAILS Marketing Group and is one of the original committee members for the Soon to be Famous Illinois Author Project. She has a BA in journalism from Northern Illinois University. A former journalist and editor, she is pursuing an MLIS degree from Dominican University. Elizabeth can be reached at lizclemmons@sbcglobal.net.

CONTRIBUTORS

JENNIFER AMLING is the digital marketing and web specialist at the Helen Plum Library in Lombard, Illinois. She has been with Helen Plum for just under ten years. She has also served as president and vice president of the LACONI (Library Administrators Conference of Northern Illinois) Outreach, Programming, and Promotion section for seven years. She has a BFA in theater arts and art history from Illinois Wesleyan University and an associate's degree in graphic design and Web design from Harper College. Jennifer enjoys learning about and working with computers and Web design, especially the Drupal and WordPress platforms. She also loves musical theater! Jennifer can be reached at jenzerbenz@gmail.com.

CHRISTINE NIELS CIGLER is the manager of public relations and outreach at the Fox River Valley Public Library District in Dundee, Illinois. She has served on the Illinois Library Association Marketing Committee and was a founding member of the RAILS Marketing Group. She has presented programs on marketing for the Illinois Library Association, the Public Library Association, and LACONI (Library Administrators Conference of Northern Illinois). She has a BA in English from the University of Illinois at Chicago and an MLIS from Dominican University. Cris can be reached at criscigler@comcast.net.

DONNA FLETCHER is the president of Donna E. Fletcher Consulting, Inc., founded in 1991. The firm works with public libraries and corporate clients to conduct market research and create strategic plans. She cochaired the Illinois Library Association Marketing Committee from 2012 to 2014, is active in the RAILS Marketing Group, and is an original member of and the author coordinator for the Soon to be Famous Illinois Author Project. Donna is a Highland Park Public Library trustee and served previously for six years, including two as board president. She has presented highly regarded programs on marketing topics at the American Library Association, Public Library Association, and Illinois Library Association conferences. Before founding her consulting practice, Donna worked at Leo Burnett Advertising (now part of Publicis) guiding strategy and advertising development for Fortune 100 clients such as Kellogg's, Pillsbury, and Procter & Gamble. She earned her BA in art history from Dartmouth College. Donna can be reached at defconsult@att.net.

ANITA QUINLAN is a community relations coordinator for the Plainfield Public Library District, which serves a community of about 70,000 people. She is active in marketing and public relations functions for the library as well as several community organizations within its service area. Her background includes teaching, sales, and marketing.

DENISE RALEIGH is the division chief of public relations and development at Gail Borden Public Library District in Elgin, Illinois. Known for bringing life-sized dinosaurs, rockets, and a live talk with an astronaut aboard the International Space Station into the library, as well as finding the funding to support those unique endeavors, she was named one of Library Journal's 2010 Mover & Shakers. She is cochair of the Illinois Library Association Advocacy Committee, a member of the RAILS Marketing Group, and a founding member of the Soon to be Famous Illinois Author Project, where she does a little of everything, including liaising with partners. Before coming to work for Gail Borden, she co-owned a small monthly publication, worked as a journalist, and practiced business law. She earned a business degree from Bowling Green State University, a Juris Doctorate from the University of Toledo, and an MSLS from Clarion University.

LUCY TARABOUR has been the adult programming and publicity coordinator for the Clarendon Hills Public Library since 2004. She received